1.00

MANAGING SENSITIVE PROJECTS

Managing Sensitive Projects

A Lateral Approach

Olivier d'Herbemont
and
Bruno César

English version adapted by
Tom Curtin and Pascal Etcheber
HERBEMONT CÉSAR & ASSOCIÉS, London and Paris

Routledge
New York

English translation © Olivier d'Herbemont, Bruno César, Tom Curtin and Pascal Etcheber 1998

All rights reserved. No part of this book may be reprinted or reproduced or utilized in any form or by any electronic, mechanical or other means, now known or hereafter invented, including photocopying and recording, or in any information storage or retrieval system, without permission in writing from the publishers.

First published as *La Stratégie du Projet Latéral* (© Dunod, 1996)

Published in 1998 by
ROUTLEDGE
29 West 35th Street
New York City, NY 10001

ISBN 0–415–92166–X

Library of Congress Cataloging-in-Publication Data
Herbemont, Olivier d'.
 [Stratégie du projet latéral. English]
 Managing sensitive projects / by Olivier d'Herbemont and Bruno César : translated by Tom Curtin and Pascal Etcheber.
    p. cm.
 Includes bibliographical references and index.
 ISBN 0–415–92166–X (hardcover)
 1. Industrial project management.   2. Psychology, Industrial.
 I. César, Bruno.   II. Title.
 HD69.P75H47 1998
 658.4'04—dc21
                                                            98–20625
                                                               CIP

This book is printed on paper suitable for recycling and made from fully managed and sustained forest sources.

Printed in Great Britain

Contents

Introduction ix

PART I BASIC CONCEPTS

1 **Characterising a Sensitive Project** 3
   Case Examples 4
   Type-1 Projects can be Managed with a Direct Strategy 9
   Type-2 Projects are Managed with an Indirect Strategy 10
   There is no Point in Overloading a Type-1 Project with a
      Strategy Adapted to a Type-2 or a Type-3 Project 11
   Points to Remember 13

2 **Segmenting the Field of Play** 15
   The Field of Play is not Fixed 15
   The Field of Play is Composed of Individuals, not Groups 17
   To Manage the Field of Play it is Vital to Segment it 18
   Points to Remember 22

3 **Measuring the Players' Sociodynamics** 23
   An Ally is neither a Friend nor an Enemy; it is Someone with
      at least as much Synergy as Antagonism 23
   The Sociodynamic Position of a Player Allows one to
      Forecast Reactions to Stimuli 27
   Points to Remember 37

4 **Lateralising the Project** 39
   Case Examples 39
   The Lateral Project 42
   Points to Remember 43

5 **Identifying Faults in the Players' Behaviour** 45
   The Magpie Syndrome 46
   The Avoidance Syndrome 50
   The Stereotype Syndrome 52
   The Frenetic Syndrome 54
   The Paralytic Syndrome 56
   The Fall Guy Syndrome 57
   Points to Remember 59

PART II LAUNCHING THE PROJECT

6 Strategies that Do Not Work — 63
The Samurai Strategy – Too Harsh — 63
Participative Strategy – Too Weak — 64
Noah's Ark – Clever but Useless — 66
Machiavelli's Strategy – Invalid by its very Principle — 68
Points to Remember — 69

7 The Strategy of the Lateral Project — 71
Sensitive Projects — 71
Only the Energy of Organised Players Counts — 74
It is Much Easier to Encourage Allies to Organise Themselves for Their Own Project – a Lateral Project — 76
Several Lateral Projects might be Necessary for the Same Project — 77
The Need for a Third Party — 78
To Create a Group Dynamic — 79
Points to Remember — 80

8 Launching the First Circle — 83
Identifying Potential Allies who are Hesitant — 83
Doing the Rounds — 84
Building a Lateral Project — 86
Organising the Launch Meeting (Revelation and Commitment) — 88
Maintaining the Dynamic — 91
Points to Remember — 93

PART III CONCEIVING A LATERAL PROJECT

9 Taking the Irrational into Account — 99
Resistance and Misunderstanding — 99
Rationalising the Irrational Using the VUD Grid — 102
Adapting a Project on Three Levels — 110
Generating Desire — 111
Giving the Project Usefulness — 114
Respecting Values — 114
Points to Remember — 118

10	**Do Not Respect Time, Respect Timing**	**119**
	Individuals do not need Time to Change, they need a Structure, a Credible 'Way Out'	119
	The Time needed to get Good Acceptance for Project is only Linked to the Capacity to Help People Rebuild Themselves	122
	Getting the Timing Right	124
	Six Techniques for 'Resynchronising' Oneself with Players – Starting off on the Right Foot	126
	Points to Remember	128
11	**Going for Broke**	**129**
	Find New Words which are Not Connected to the Past and which Describe What is About to be Done in Concrete Terms	129
	Avoid Imperceptible Change	132
	Points to Remember	133
12	**Have Allies Write the Lateral Project**	**135**
	Allies are More Convinced if they Discover the Arguments to Convince Themselves	135
	Everything that is Said will, without doubt, be Marked with a Strong Source Effect	136
	Points to Remember	137
13	**Moving from Penalties to Benefits**	**139**
	Sanctions and Antagonism	139
	Rewards	140
	Points to Remember	141

PART IV DEVELOPING THE DYNAMICS OF THE LATERAL PROJECT

14	**Helping Allies to Act**	**145**
	The Difficulty with Helping	145
	Establishing an Efficient Help Relationship	146
	Paving the Way for Action with Methodological Support	149
	Helping to Identify Allies	149
	Helping to Reach Agreement	152
	Helping to Plan Actions	154
	Helping to Form a Concrete Vision of the Future	156
	Points to Remember	161

Contents

15 Adapting a Project in Real Time According to Events and Micro-Events — 163
A Common Language: the Significant Facts or Micro-Events — 163
Knowing of Events Preferably in Advance — 166
To Manage an Event is to Adapt it or to Adapt the Project — 168
Making Systematic Direct Contact with the Players — 171
Developing Non-media Channels — 174
Implementing Animation Systems — 177
Points to Remember — 178

16 Ensuring the Management Team's Solidarity — 181
Strengthening the Project Manager — 182
Strengthening the Database — 185
Issuing Reference Documents that are Consensual — 189
Points to Remember — 191

PART V   MANAGING THOSE WHO OPPOSE A LATERAL PROJECT

17 Check Whether a Player is Truly an Opponent — 195

18 When Tension is Rising, Master the 'Daggers-Drawn' Phase — 197

19 Fight Opponents without being Obsessed by Them: The 'Price of Fish' Response — 199

20 Individualise Responses: The 'Horace and Curiace' Strategy — 205

21 Do not be Lured into the Trap of an Adversarial Debate — 207

22 Remain the White Knight: Make Allies Attack — 209
Points to Remember — 210

CONCLUSION: SIX KEYS TO SUCCESS

1. Have a Project — 211
2. Accept the Need to Rethink One's Personal Project — 212
3. Favour the Individual rather than the Group — 212
4. Favour Actions — 212
5. Take into Account the Fears of Others — 213
6. Bet on Goodwill — 213

Bibliography — 215
Glossary — 217
Index — 225

Introduction

We live in paradoxical times.

Every day, managers must adapt to rapidly changing markets and situations. Consultants fall in line and propose ever more radical new models for change.

Yet change has never been more difficult. Every day new rules and regulations add to that difficulty.

And when change becomes essential, few dare tackle it for fear of total rejection, or worse, to see it drown in a sea of committees and waffle.

Yet it is the nature of people to resist change even when they benefit from it. That is the paradox. But the world cannot stand still. There are important infrastructural projects ranging from new roads and airports to reforms of the health and education services and all will be resisted.

Companies, too, face these problems. Every day it seems that twice as much productivity is needed from half the number of staff at a quarter of the price. New ways of working, re-engineering, complex new IT systems, all need to be introduced to people who will resist them.

This book deals with these sensitive or difficult projects. They range from redundancy programmes to the disposal of radioactive waste. From the launch of new products to the introduction of a new computer system – in other words, change in sensitive areas and in difficult times.

The method – the strategy of the lateral project – is radically different from those used in projects which are normally associated with traditional project management. It is derived from twenty years of experience working with brave managers on projects which many others would have left to their successors.

The strategy of the lateral project in essence is a way of introducing change by having an understanding of people and why they act in certain ways, by being flexible and by looking for allies rather than attacking enemies. If it sounds simple, then it is. But pick up your newspaper and see how often common sense is the first casualty in a sensitive project.

When a manager first embarks on change, even if it is for the common good, he or she cannot know precisely how people will react. 'Educated guesses' will be made, but too often one is not prepared for the strength of reaction. How often does one hear: 'If I had known it was going to turn out like that, I wouldn't have bothered.' Too often important initiatives die because managers know they will lead to their own downfall.

And yet there is often little that divides the sides. But entrenched positions are quickly found and taken. Small details become major issues. Now it's 'us' or 'them'.

The lateral project is one which is 'us' and 'them'. For the project promoter or manager, it means flexibility, an ability to listen and change – often our own deeply-ingrained beliefs – and the understanding that one cannot do everything on one's own, even if the biggest company in the world is leading the project.

There are three guiding principles:

- **People are too quickly labelled as friends or foes.** But, misunderstandings can quickly arise. The words we use do not inevitably have the same meaning for everyone. This is true even if the listener is from our country, from our background, from our environment or from our company.
- **Managers lock themselves into a stereotyped model of the world dominated by struggles with opponents.** But our experience shows that one is surrounded by people who could support the project if only they could be mobilised and if they were spoken to with the right form of words.
- **Managers take on too much: they try to impose the project by making themselves personally indispensable.** However, experience shows that it is never a single action from the head of the project, however good and courageous that action may be, through which a sensitive project can succeed. It is not enough to have right on your side.

The essence of managing a sensitive project is to mobilise the allies, even if they do not look like allies at the first glance. It is their co-ordinated action and dynamism – through **their** (lateral) project, which they have adapted and adopted – which will convince the rest of the population.

Introduction xi

The case histories are drawn from practical experience and from real life. In some instances, names and circumstances have been changed in order to preserve the anonymity of individual people and companies.

We hope that this book will bring courage and ideas to those brave managers who tackle difficult and sensitive projects which less courageous managers would either ignore or bypass.

Part I
Basic Concepts

'There's many a slip 'twixt the cup and the lip', according to the old proverb.

In the usual sense, a project is simply an intention to do something. In this book, little focus is given to the final purpose of a project. This will be taken for granted. Whether a project makes sense, whether it is timely, good or even required will not be questioned: other people will do that.

However, sensitive or difficult projects – which are the subject of this book – are more than just intentions. These projects also take into account the coordinated actions by the key players which are needed in order to achieve the success of the project.

It is the actions of real people, within the framework of a project, which leads to its success or failure. These people are called 'key players' or 'players' – a term first used by the sociologist Crozier – to differentiate them from 'spectators' who make up the rest of the population. The focus must be on the players as it is they who can make or break a sensitive project.

In traditional project management there are three key areas: the project, the actions needed, and the key players. These three areas are not adequate to describe the management of sensitive projects, and there are five extra concepts which will be used throughout the book. The first part of the book defines these concepts which are:

- *Concept 1* characterising a sensitive project;
- *Concept 2* segmenting the field of play;
- *Concept 3* measuring the players' sociodynamics;
- *Concept 4* lateralising the project;
- *Concept 5* identifying faults in the players' behaviour.

1 Characterising a Sensitive Project

In 20 years of professional experience the authors have been confronted with many projects, all of them falling into the 'sensitive' category.

It has become clear that there are two kinds of difficulties in a project: technical difficulties and human difficulties. The way to manage a project varies profoundly depending on which type of project it is. Human difficulties arise because some of the people who have an involvement in the project do not want to do what is expected of them or are strongly opposed to what is asked of them.

Figure 1.1 is used to study and characterise the types of projects involving change working on the principle that this can be measured along two axes.

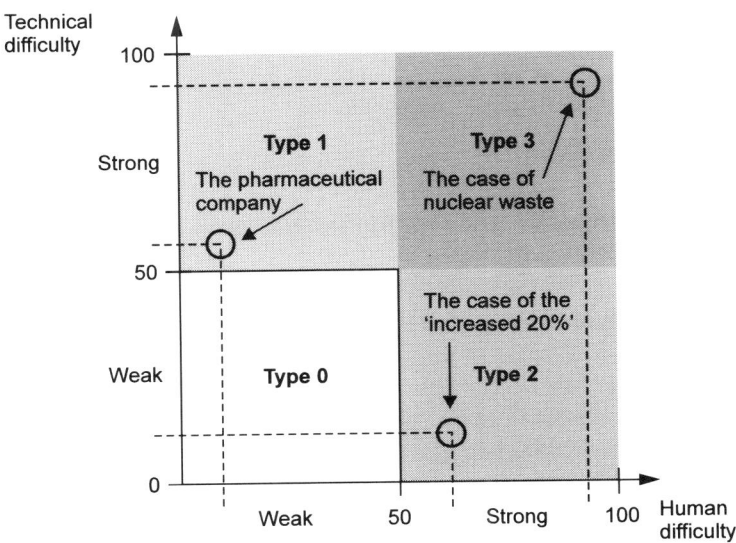

Figure 1.1 Types of projects

The y-axis indicates technical difficulty. There are many factors which increase that difficulty:

- technological innovation and the way it is utilised;
- the number of people involved;
- the time-scale of the project;
- the number of stages before completion;
- the financial investment;
- the risks in the event of failure.

The x-axis indicates human difficulty: this is evaluated by measuring the number of allies and the number of opponents to the project. Later in the book it will be shown how sociodynamics allows this scale to be measured more precisely.

This simple diagram identifies three main types of projects (we may ignore the Type 0 project which simply reflects normal change within a company and so does not deserve much attention):

- *Type 1 projects* are very difficult technically but are rarely subject to human difficulties;
- *Type 2 projects*, by contrast, are prone to human difficulties but not to technical ones;
- *Type 3 projects* blend all these difficulties – the technical and human – a true nightmare!

CASE EXAMPLES

The following examples will help to illustrate each type.

A Type 1 Project: The Pharmaceutical Company

This case represents a very technical project. A wholesaler of pharmaceuticals, located in a provincial city, has two warehouses, one in the city centre and the other in an industrial zone. Rapidly increasing sales lead the company's management to believe it will soon need a third warehouse. A firm of consultants specialising in logistics is called in to evaluate the situation.

The experts visit both warehouses, talk to the managers, make their calculations and arrive at a surprising conclusion: there is no need to create a third warehouse. On the contrary, the company should close the one in the city centre. The warehouse in the industrial zone, with some modifications, will largely meet existing and future needs. Whereas the client was looking to three warehouses, the experts recommend only one. The savings will be measured in millions.

The solution is so obviously attractive and simple that the consulting firm is asked to oversee the transfer. There will be no layoffs, the local council has agreed, the management applauds and the staff rejoices.

The consultants work out a precise analysis of the volumes and numbers of stocks and their movements. They draw up the logistical requirements for the new warehouse and organise tenders for the different suppliers. They finalise a detailed plan of the new warehouse containing the position and space allocation for each of the company's 30 000 products.

The consultants then write the operational procedures manuals for the new work-flow, sketch the transfer maps of activities from one warehouse to the other and train the staff on the new procedures. Thousands of tasks which have to be executed are precisely nested into each other. Managed one by one, they form a 'machine' with the precision of a Swiss watch.

Everything is planned, and everything happens as planned. During a memorable weekend the stock is moved from the city centre and assimilated into the new layout in the single warehouse. From pharmaceuticals to diapers, the 30 000 products are moved one by one and are installed between Friday night and Monday morning.

D-day. At eight o'clock on the Monday morning, the warehouse starts and the system functions without a hitch. The crisis team, whose role is to manage possible malfunctions, complains it has nothing to do. The investment is returned in six months; the company has become a case study for the sector; people come from other countries to visit the new installations. The dream has become a reality.

Examples of projects of this type abound, in principle at least, and study groups and consulting firms are stacked with them, from the launch of a television channel specialising in round-the-clock news to the construction of an oil platform.

Evaluation

- *Technical difficulty*: quite strong. There are three reasons for this: the number of products to manage individually; the novelty of computer programming for managing orders, and the risk of chemists being out of stock should the move be delayed. The project is rated at 60 per cent.
- *Human difficulty*: almost nil, besides the need to motivate those who are in charge of filling in orders. It is rated at 10 per cent.

A Type 2 Project: The Case of the 'Increased 20%'

A state-owned industrial firm is driven by a board of high-ranking civil servants. It is heavily unionised and has a strong culture dominated by the employees' right to a job for life. For economic reasons, it has been decided that the company needs to increase productivity by 20 per cent.

The board decides that the best way to achieve this is by introducing a third shift, working at night. This should be technically simple, especially as the third night shift had previously existed a few years before. In other words, all the systems of remuneration, procedures and work organisations already exist.

But there is a problem: as a matter of principle the unions are opposed to night working. The staff are also against the change, even if it is sweetened with bonuses, as they are assured of a job and have a comfortable salary.

The authors are brought in to work on the project and are met with a stalemate. On the one hand the management is unwilling to move, and on the other hand the staff is not willing to change. It is obvious that management has no power, or hardly any, over the staff, except a meagre ability to cause nuisance that it already utilises excessively. Paralysed by the huge power of the unions, the board systematically begins to disown the management and to go back on its decisions. Finally, being accustomed to this back-tracking, the management loses all confidence in the board

For the authors it is clear that one must first motivate the managers and the board (the general administrative directors, the high-ranking civil servants, etc.) rather than try to get any change accepted by the staff and the unions. A thorough diagnosis of the working relationships within the company is recommended. This is readily accepted by the board as they see the diagnosis as a technical analysis, with which they are comfortable. It will allow the relationships between management and staff to be unravelled as well as gaining an understanding of the key players and their strategies. In addition, it will be a first step towards making those who are taking part in the exercise face change.

During a very tense meeting the evidence forcibly strikes the board: working relationships at the heart of the company must be changed. The problem of the third shift is no longer the issue. The important issue is the poor structure which caused the problem in the first place.

This analysis – which focuses on the working relationships between individuals – is presented to middle management and to the whole staff. Work groups are put in place with the unions, not on the subject of a third shift, but on the subject of the future of the company. In parallel, a separate project is launched with the most motivated managers and supervisors to find improved work practices to achieve the required 20 per cent productivity increase.

In time, a majority of the management accepts the need for a third shift. Other topics, not mentioned until now, are introduced and dealt with. The most difficult sectors are analysed. The management team, now reconstituted and showing solidarity, finds a solution for each problem. Little by little the project begins to come together.

In parallel, work continues on the human relationship problems within the company. Some unions try to break this project but fail: there is no appetite for a strike. A year after the beginning of the process the unions sign an agreement which includes the creation of a third shift and the launch of a consultation on early retirement, overmanning and retraining for new skills.

Evaluation

- *Technical difficulty*: weak. As mentioned, the third shift already existed a few years ago and the tools for remuneration, procedures and work organisation were in place previously. It is rated at 10 per cent.
- *Human difficulty*: very strong. What is striking is not so much the number of opponents, but the severe lack of allies. It is rated at 70 per cent.

A Type 3 Project: The Case of Nuclear Waste

EPA is a French state-owned company with the task of managing nuclear waste. It has a specific objective to find a safe place for the underground storage of long-lived, high-level wastes.

In 1991, EPA's staff identified some sites that were technically and geologically well-suited. However, further investigations were needed and when the engineers and scientists arrived at the sites with their drilling rigs there was local uproar. The police were called and the army was mobilised in order to let the work proceed. Yet, within weeks, the sheer force of local opposition forced EPA to withdraw. This very rational approach to the project led to a social explosion. The outcome: the project was totally stopped and most of the management team was replaced.

EPA then changed its strategy. First, it decided to stop all investigative work for two years. (It will be seen later that this is one of the basic tools of the management of a sensitive project.) This allowed the key players to reorganise themselves and let the tensions diminish.

Second, at the end of 1991 a mediation mission was formed which was headed by a member of parliament reputed for his approachability. He first contacted all the people who might be concerned with the project: members of parliament, heads of political parties, local councils, environmentalists, etc., in order to get an understanding of the project. From these initial contacts he drafted a piece of legislation which was laid before the French legislature. The legislation, which took into account the prime concerns of most people, was passed by a good majority of the Assembly. The law incorporated some strong guarantees which allowed elected representatives and interested groups, such as environmentalists, access to the decision-making process. It also included financial incentives for those communities which would be considered as a location for the storage site.

The government then asked the same member of parliament to embark on a new mission to explain the aims of the law to interested parties and to receive applications (on a voluntary basis) from communities which might wish to have a storage site within their boundaries. In a very informal manner he contacted each of France's 100 departments and the elected representatives. If he sensed a degree of interest for the project in an area he made an official presentation, but, it should again be stressed, only to those departments which showed an interest.

Following these presentations, some communities voluntarily came forward. These were then assessed confidentially by EPA's engineers for their technical and geological suitability. (It is worth noting again the overlap of political problems and technical problems.)

From the volunteer sites only four had the potential technical attributes. These were selected for further investigation so allowing the project to resume.

Evaluation

- *Technical difficulty*: considerable. This project possesses the whole spectrum of technical difficulties: financial stakes (billions), technological uncertainties, the number of players involved and the length of the process.
- *Human difficulty*: considerable. The word nuclear sums it up – it can be explosive. Parallels can be drawn with big issues like the death penalty, AIDS or mad cow disease. All these subjects provoke strong reactions and the adoption of fixed and hostile stances, leaving little room for rational and calm analysis.

Through these three examples, it can be seen that the implementation strategy must be adapted to the type of project. Indeed, the type of project conditions the strategy to be implemented.

TYPE 1 PROJECTS CAN BE MANAGED WITH A DIRECT STRATEGY

In general, the strategy for Type 1 projects can be summed up as a trade-off between deadlines, costs and objectives. This direct strategy can be best explained using military terms borrowed from Clausewitz, the 20th century Prussian war strategist. He said:

> One attacks when one is the strongest. In that case, one mobilises the maximum forces in a minimum of time against the strongest points of the enemy. One shatters the enemy and then everything else follows.

Direct strategy gives all its power to planners and logistics experts: the battle is not won while it is being fought, it is won before it has started.

Whoever launches the project has the power, the troops follow; the responsibility is to organise everyone's role in order for the battle to be won. The challenge is to distribute responsibilities, to define minutely the workload and everyone's objectives.

The mastery of a Type 1 project requires the existence of a clearly identified project leader, whose main role consists of telling people what they have to do and coordinating them. In fact, the other key players demand this. This centralisation of coordination does not mean that the players have no freedom to act, but that freedom can only express itself through the framework of the project.

A Type 1 project is dominated by 'tasks'. *The implementation strategy consists of logically structuring the project in successive tasks whose sum leads to the ultimate objective sought*, of allocating the resources to the tasks and controlling any slippage or deviation from the programme.

The human element is not really taken into account except for two variables:

- *their quantity*: three hundred man days are needed for a month, for example; and
- *their skills*: a design engineer and a lawyer are needed.

Of course, there are always those within the team who do not fully support the project, but they tend to be scattered and count for little in its ultimate success or failure. The Type 1 project is a classic case from books on management theory. This type of project management is a well-developed area and there is little to be added on the methods and precautions to be taken to ensure success, except to follow precisely the established rules. These types of projects are not the subject of this book.

TYPE 2 PROJECTS ARE MANAGED WITH AN INDIRECT STRATEGY

Using the direct strategy with Type 2 or Type 3 projects has disadvantages and can lead to problems.

The predominance of Clausewitzian thinking led to the bloody trench battles of the First World War. After the exhausting conflicts of the Somme and Flanders, when it became apparent that this strategy led to stalemate, an English author, B. H. Liddell Hart, disagreed with Clausewitz. He said: 'The war strategy must reduce fighting to the smallest amount possible by attacking the line of least resistance and the line of least expectation'.

The theory was refined by Lyautey, who was French Minister for War in 1917–18. He formulated a new approach which said: 'When using armed forces, avoid the column as much as possible and replace it with progressive occupation'. This strategy is well-adapted to sensitive projects.

Indirect strategy is related to this theory and was used in the case of the 'Increased 20%' discussed above. It starts from the principle that opponents are like seeds that only grow in certain places. The surest way to fight them is to make the ground (that is, the people) hostile.

In a project which involves human complexity, the focus is not on what has to be done (on tasks), but on the players who will perform or will not perform those tasks, or who will prevent those tasks from being carried out. To succeed in the implementation of a sensitive project on a human level, one has to change the map, in the same way that military strategists have changed models. To throw oneself into a sensitive project with a blueprint and a fixed budget is as foolish as travelling to India with a map of Brazil.

THERE IS NO POINT IN OVERLOADING A TYPE 1 PROJECT WITH A STRATEGY ADAPTED TO A TYPE 2 OR A TYPE 3 PROJECT

At the beginning of any project the dilemma is always the same: is a direct or an indirect strategy needed? Is it a Type 1 or Type 2 project? It is easy to gauge the situation afterwards!

To use a direct strategy with a Type 2 or Type 3 project is certainly a mistake. On the contrary, a project that is by its very nature Type 1 will benefit from being managed with a direct strategy because it is more economical and has the added advantage of clearly defining the objective.

Too often one sees Type 1 projects being managed with a strategy adapted to sensitive projects. Often the reason is that the top management has no project; it merely has a problem and does not know how to, or does not want to, find a solution. So, it expects the players to find the way. Much social and industrial unrest can be caused by top management not having real projects, but only having the desire to get rid of a problem.

> ### A Project of Type 1 Managed with a Strategy of Type 2: The Case of the Distribution Company
>
> The chairman of a distribution company calls the authors after filing for protection from his creditors under the Bankruptcy Act. He wants to devise a plan to rescue the company by using a participative method, based on consensus.
>
> A methodical plan is devised using the very best practice to generate the maximum amount of consensus. Three months later the facts become clear: although technically complex and delicate, the solutions to be implemented generate no suspicion or opposition. Everyone is waiting expectantly for a word from top management to spring them into action.
>
> Of course employees are very worried about redundancies, but are fully aware that the company cannot survive as it is. All signs indicate that any opposition to the plans will be short-lived and opponents cannot undermine the project. But, instead of making a decision, the top management wants everyone to 'participate', they 'ask the staff for advice', they debate, query, question, but decide nothing. As a result of the process, some detailed improvements are obtained, but the company is not back on its feet, though it could have been.
>
> **Evaluation**
>
> - *Technical difficulty*: average. It seems that the top management is not competent and does not know how to pinpoint strategic improvements. However, whoever takes over the company will be able to make it profitable in a year. It is rated at 60 per cent.
> - *Human difficulty*: weak. In this case, as in all company rescues, top management has the formidable power to say: 'This is it, accept it or else I close'. Experience shows that in this type of situation staff accept all the sacrifices once they have been clearly explained. Yet, the staff need to feel the decisiveness of the top management, they need to trust its technical ability, and the tasks and responsibilities have to be clearly distributed.

POINTS TO REMEMBER

- Implementation strategies have to be adopted which suit each type of project.
- To adopt a Type 2 strategy for a Type 1 project considerably overloads the process and leads to missed deadlines and increased costs.
- A Type 1 strategy applied to a Type 2 or Type 3 project can provoke a strong backlash.

Just because there is a human or social conflict, this alone does not categorise a project as Type 2 or Type 3. The social conflict may merely reveal the absence of a real project.

2 Segmenting the Field of Play

The implementation strategy for a sensitive project is characterised by the fact that one is first interested in the key players before being interested in the tasks to be carried out. As a matter of fact there is no point in defining what has to be done if there is no one to do it.

For a technical project the human aspects are easy: one starts by listing the tasks and then organises them in a plan. By contrast, with a sensitive project the first stage is to list the players and measure their potential contributions to the project. A field of play is designed and defined within which the key players can be active.

THE FIELD OF PLAY IS NOT FIXED

In theory, nothing is simpler than to draw up the field of play for a project. It defines itself. A building is to be constructed? The key players are the local government, the suppliers, the potential customers. A new information system is to be introduced? The players are the computer suppliers and the users. The university has to expand? The players are the professors, the students, the administrative staff, the unions, and the local community.

However, defining the field of play always throws up surprises. One starts by working very calmly on a clean sheet of paper on a flip-chart. Soon there are ten sheets stuck on the wall of the meeting room, each filled with arrows, crosses and question marks. At the end of the day, there are still unanswered questions.

However, this is a good sign: it means that those responsible for the project are beginning to recognise those people who will have to be convinced of its merits. More often than not, only those who impose themselves are considered as key players whilst others – whose usefulness is underestimated – are forgotten. It is easier to identify potential opponents than potential allies.

A Field of Play Badly Managed: The Newbury By-Pass

The ports of Southampton and Portsmouth in the South of England are two of the busiest in Britain. They provide vital links for exports from the Midlands and the North of the country to mainland Europe. Similarly imports from France and Spain also pass through the ports.

The road which links the ports to the North is the A34. An important trunk road, it is a dual-carriageway – except at Newbury, where it almost passes through the town centre. Plans for by-pass around this historical market town were first mooted in the 1950s. But plans came and went and nothing happened until the late 1980s when a public inquiry decided that a new road should be built to the West of the town rather than to the East. This divided the local community.

After a number of false starts, work began and then direct action environmentalists moved in and occupied the trees on the site. Security guards were called, the police were called and the place looked like a battle ground. In fact, one of the major battles of the English civil war was fought at Newbury and people began to make comparisons.

The delays over the months and the demonstrations were expensive and time-consuming. But during all the time, the opponents grabbed the centre stage. Although the local MP spoke out for the road as local traffic conditions were appalling, his voice was almost drowned out.

But many other allies were not heard at all. Those local people who took two hours to get to the supermarket on bad traffic days never organised themselves to speak out. But equally importantly, the elected representatives of Portsmouth and Southampton, their parliamentarians, their chambers of commerce, their leaders were all silent.

Evaluation

The field of play had been reduced to those who forced themselves on to it. Those who were potential direct beneficiaries – the people of Newbury and the cities of Portsmouth and Southampton – were hardly heard during the conflict. The road – still under guard – is under construction. The protesters moved to Manchester Airport to try to stop the building of a second runway.

Segmenting the Field of Play 17

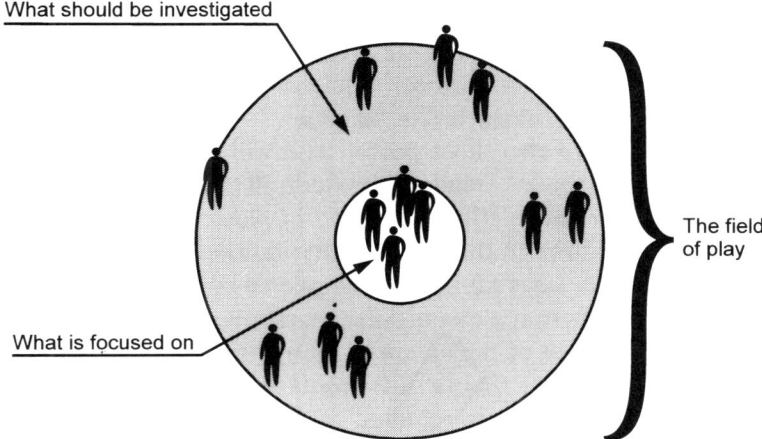

Figure 2.1 The main failing is to let players, often opponents, force themselves on a project, and not search for more helpful players

As we have seen, there is a natural tendency not to search for other players but to deal solely with those who force themselves on the project (see Figure 2.1). These important players who are ignored could decide to remain as spectators, or worse, could fail to realise how useful they could be.

By definition, if a project is sensitive it is because the players who occupy the field of play are likely to be opposed to the project. Consequently, the search for allies in a different field of play becomes as important a strategic objective as how to win their support. The search for key players outside the traditional areas is one of the real areas of freedom in a sensitive project.

The successful implementation of a sensitive project is as much about changing the players as it is about changing how they act.

THE FIELD OF PLAY IS COMPOSED OF INDIVIDUALS, NOT GROUPS

So, the project is not a formal organisation, it is a group of people some being more involved than others, with only a proportion taking actions and being organised.

First there are those who are responsible for undertaking the project, called the 'project team'. Then there are those who have an institutional role such as planning authorities, regulatory bodies whose legitimate function it is to place 'obstacles' in the way

But the players are also those people who will either benefit or suffer from the project. If this is extended to include all those who could have an influence on the project, defining the field of play becomes a rather vast and complex operation. In the Newbury By-Pass case, one could define a field of play that includes all the French people and many Europeans.

The first instinct is to use quantitative market research. But this flawed reasoning is at the root of the failure of many projects. This theory relies on statistics and assumes that in order to understand the likely reactions of a population, all that is required is to test a significant sample. However, the challenge is not to know what people in general think but to mobilise particular individuals. A field of players is composed of individuals, not of 'statistical groups', 'hierarchic levels' or 'social-economic types'.

TO MANAGE THE FIELD OF PLAY IT IS VITAL TO SEGMENT IT

To define a field of play by drawing up a simple list of key players is not sufficient: to manage a sensitive project, it must be manageable. The basic means of doing this is to segment it into sub-sections. This principle is as old as time and comes from the needs of those in authority to master numerous and diverse groups of people in order to get them to work together. The principle consists of gathering people into homogenous groups of a 'human size', and ensuring that there is a representative of authority in each group.

Roman legions were segmented into groups of a hundred with a centurion in charge in order to ease manoeuvres. The Christian church is structured in parishes with a vicar or priest. Most countries are segmented into smaller administrative areas – councils or departments – which in turn are segmented further into districts or communes.

Trade unions segment the company in order to control the many militants scattered throughout the workforce. They segment the company into 'sectors' (see Figure 2.2) that reflect its basic structure: administrative offices, the warehouse, the computer room, the shop floor, and so on. Each sector meets two criteria: first, it can be 'managed' by a single person, which means that the union officer responsible for a sector can

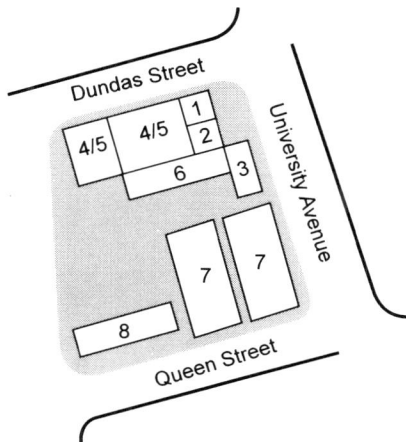

Figure 2.2 The segmentation of a company by work areas

quickly get to know each employee on a first-name basis. Second, a sector is easy to understand and is homogenous: a 'welder' is not asked to take care of the administrative office.

Of course the union does not approach all sectors at once. It starts with the areas with the strongest number of allies (see Figure 2.3). For each sector someone is made responsible and is called the collector or shop steward, since every month these people traditionally collect the union dues. Each month there is an opportunity to find out about grievances, to persuade waverers to join the union and to update lists (see Figure 2.4).

So, every month, the union has:

- an exact understanding of its standing within the company; and
- the state of grievances.

If, in any given month, there is a fall-off in membership in a particular sector, a senior union official will visit it to try to ascertain if there any problems. Once the union has representatives in those sectors of the company in which it has support, it attacks another area which is geographically close or which is undergoing change.

As can be seen from this simple example, 'segmenting the field of play' means that one not only knows intimately, and on an individual basis, the opinions of the players regarding the project; it also serves as a mechanism to test the quality of the contact: is there one trustworthy person in each sector who can maintain contact with the players?

Basic Concepts

	Sector 1	Sector 2	Sector 3	Sector 4
	Customer service	Reception	Computer room	Drivers (a.m.)
Personnel	11	5	12	32
Allies	1	1	0	0
Opponents	2	0	2	6
	Sector 5	Sector 6	Sector 7	Sector 8
	Drivers (p.m.)	Office administration	Entrance gate	Quality control
Personnel	37	20	12	8
Allies	3	12	2	8
Opponents	4	0	1	0

Figure 2.3 Identifying the allies

Project: Change of shift pattern Sector: Drivers Project manager: Steve Douglas					
Who	Ally	Opponent	?	To do	
Lubbock, Liz	×			Ask the secretaries	
Barry, James			×	Go and see him	
Feagan, Michael		×		Nothing	
Smith, Carol	×			Go and see him	
Turner, Matthew		×		Nothing	
Hudson, Harry	×			Needs support	
Ross, Miles			×	Ask James	
O'Connor, Jim			×	Go and see him	
Pickett, Sarah	×			Phone Mrs Jones	

Figure 2.4 Segmenting the field of play

The Result of Segmenting the Field of Play in a Pensions Company

A pensions company wants to renegotiate its terms of employment and introduce a new system of remuneration based on performance. To prepare for this, the chief executive segments the field of play. The company is spread over six floors. It quickly becomes clear that on two floors there has traditionally been strong opposition to all changes. There are no allies to whom the company can delegate the task of explaining the new system.

Before announcing anything, the chief executive decides to change one of the department heads who is competent but not reliable. He also moves an administrative service to one of the floors with few allies. Once this segmenting of the area is completed, the project is announced. The new contacts which have been put in place function perfectly. True communication is established. Reform goes smoothly with only a few detailed modifications.

This example shows that the segmentation of the field of play does not distinguish between collecting information and action. *Segmenting the field of play is not just a means of knowing the ground but also a way to act on the ground.*

This last point is important. It contradicts classical marketing thinking, which is a highly segmented process, in that:

- a specialist undertakes a market research study;
- from this study, the product development executive develops a product; and then
- the sales executive sells the product to those who took part in the original market research.

In a sensitive project, to ask questions, to inform oneself of the opinion of the players is already an action that can provoke a chain reaction. Evaluating the field of play from the participant's point of view, allows thorough segmentation to take into account the link between ascending and descending information.

POINTS TO REMEMBER

- There is a tendency to let players be imposed on a project either through inertia or a lack of openness.
- One must know how to find new players outside the normal or traditional field of a project and to ignore others who impose themselves.
- It is dangerous to limit oneself to a 'statistical' vision of the players. One must have a means of keeping in contact with each player individually.
- To manage the field of play it is vital to segment it.
- In order to evaluate the dynamics of a field of play, one must have a means of evaluating the quality of how one has segmented it.

3 Measuring the Players' Sociodynamics

Segmenting the field of play allows the individual identification of those players who could act for or against a project. But what does it mean: 'to act for or against a project?' How can one say that somebody is an ally or an opponent? This is a fundamental question since everyone agrees that one cannot treat a friend or a foe in the same way. How one characterises the players, whether it is implicit or explicit, is therefore a key element of the strategy.

The classical approach is too simplistic to be of any use. In the airforce there is a system called 'friend or foe' to identify automatically whether one is facing a friendly aircraft or an enemy aircraft. In the heat of battle it is crucial to be able to ask directly: 'whose side are you on?'

In most cases, however, life is a bit more complicated – even in military matters. In the Gulf War, was Syria a friend or an enemy of the United States? If it was not an ally, neither was it an enemy: it was an 'objective ally', as the journalists put it. In the same way, to limit one's analysis of politics to right and left is too simplistic.

With sensitive projects, classifying people into friends or enemies, although natural, is not effective. To trust one's *feelings*, or the assessments of those of a player's colleagues, is a risky way of evaluating attitudes to the project. How can one be unbiased in those areas? How can one acquire a common language between the members of the team in order to agree who is an ally and who is an opponent? Jean-Christian Fauvet, one of the founding fathers of sociodynamics, proposed a simple and efficient tool to measure with precision the level of involvement of a player in a project and to identify allies dispassionately.

AN ALLY IS NEITHER A FRIEND NOR AN ENEMY; IT IS SOMEONE WITH AT LEAST AS MUCH SYNERGY AS ANTAGONISM

The idea behind sociodynamics is simple. Let's forget complex grids that try to describe the sociology of organisations and the psychology of players. Let's focus on what brings about change: the energy that the

24   Basic Concepts

players devote to the project. *To be precise, let's concentrate on the energy that each player devotes to a project.*

First, players fall into two camps: those who expend a lot of energy on a project and those who do not expend much energy. Experience shows that the latter are generally by far the more numerous, between 40 per cent and 80 per cent of a given population on any given subject.

Then let's look at the nature of that energy. 'Synergy' is the energy that a player develops (or which can be developed) to support a project. 'Antagonism' is the energy that a player develops against a project.

The second contribution of sociodynamics is that it allows someone to be both synergetic and antagonistic for a given project. In fact sociodynamics allows different players to be mapped on the same diagram, with their contributions to the project measured as synergy on the y-axis and antagonism on the x-axis (see Figure 3.1)

This is a considerable improvement on the classical approach. It allows one to combine the fact that an individual is more or less for or against the project, but also whether or not he or she is involved in the action. That allows one to understand better what happens in the hinterland between 'those for' and 'those against'.

How can the synergy and antagonism of a player be measured? Fauvet proposes separate scales of measurement for synergy and antagonism. Taking synergy first, this is measured on a scale from +1 to +4. Let's first segment the players into two categories, those who take initiatives for the project and those who do not (see Figure 3.2). *Initiative is the capacity to act in favour of the project without being asked.*

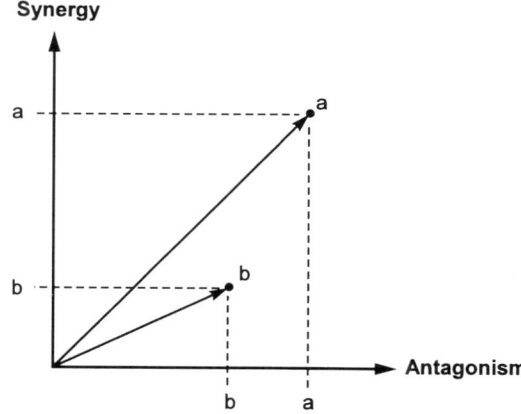

Figure 3.1   A player can be both synergetic and antagonistic for the project and exhibit different levels

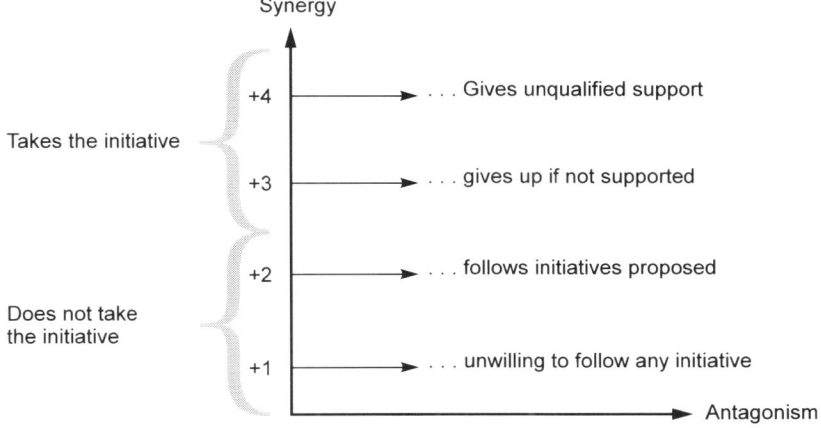

Figure 3.2 How to measure the synergy of a player

Taking the Initiative at a Dinner Party

At a dinner party, one guest says: 'I am writing a book on how to succeed with sensitive projects'. Clearly this is his main focus in life at the moment.

The person on his right says: 'How interesting! I hope you will give me a copy once it is finished'.

The person on his left says: 'If you are interested, I could arrange for you to meet Mr X who has some interesting things to say on this subject'.

Evaluation

The person on the right shows a certain amount of synergy since he shows an interest in the project, but he does not take any initiative to help the author progress. His request for a free copy of the book shows a certain amount of antagonism since he is actually taking away some energy and some money from the author.

The person on the left does not seem to have much interest in his proposal. Yet, he proves to have a far greater amount of synergy than the person on the right since he is taking the initiative of proposing a useful meeting which will help the author with the book. He is going to devote energy to help the project succeed.

Most players do not bring much energy to a project, they are more likely to take energy from it. Others have much synergy, they show initiative. Nothing is asked of them, but when the project is mentioned they alone take the initiative to propose something which will help. There are two levels among those who take initiatives: there is initiative and initiative! Those who take an initiative but give up when they are not followed up are considered separately from those who take an initiative and who keep on taking the initiative without prompting.

The mark +3 is given to a player who takes initiatives but who needs to be encouraged in order to continue. The mark +4 is given to those who do not need to be encouraged to continue to support the project. So, in the example of the dinner party there are two possible conclusions. One is that the author has to remind the person on the right about his offer: 'You mentioned that I should meet Mr X, is that still possible?' The person on the right is rated +3. Or, the author forgets the meeting and two days later he receives a telephone call from the guest saying: 'I was very interested by our conversation the day before yesterday. Are you still interested in meeting Mr X?' That person is then rated +4.

But what of those who do not take initiatives? Their synergy is not very strong but it needs to be clarified. There are different ways of being passive. We give the rating +2 to those who do not take any initiative but who follow those that are proposed to them. For example, they are asked: 'Could you read my manuscript?' and they will answer: 'With pleasure!' They have no energy: it would never occur to them to take the initiative nor do they have the willingness to do so, but they are ready to do what is asked of them.

Those who unwillingly follow our initiatives, and who need to be reminded many times, get the rating +1. It's worth noting that those who come to meetings, even if only to say that they did not want to come, are following the initiative of the organiser and they rate +2 even if they show a strong level of antagonism. Obviously, a player who never follows an initiative for a project, even when reminded many times, will rate 0.

Turning to the antagonism of a player towards a project, this is measured on a scale of -1 to -4. The antagonism of an individual is the energy expended in order to get a competing project to succeed (see Figure 3.3). However, this project might just be a variant of the original project. For example, the director of a computing department wanted to computerise the sales force immediately, while the network director favoured a period of manual operation in order to ensure that the change would bring benefits and to take time to isolate problems.

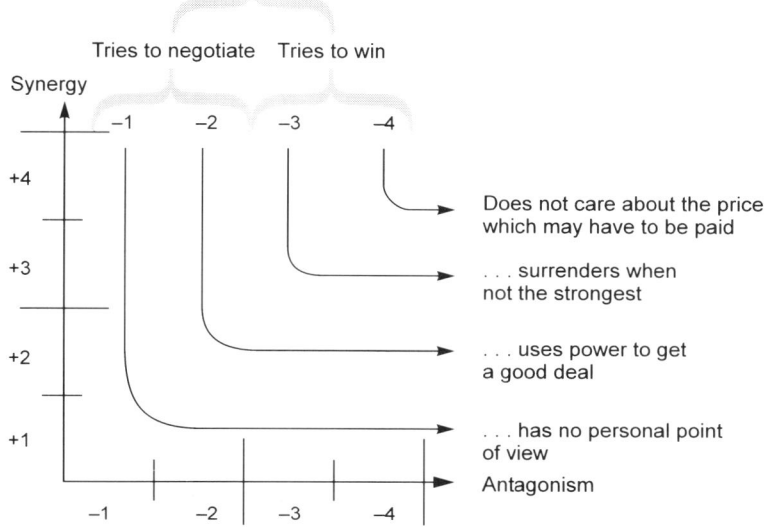

Figure 3.3 How to measure the antagonism of a player

But a competitive project may have no linkage. For example, a marketing manager who is enthusiastic for the introduction of a new computer system as it will improve his direct mail data-bases may turn against it when fresh costings are introduced. The increased price means there is no budget for an important advertising campaign proposed by the marketing department.

A person with no competing project is rated at −1. If an individual has a competing project but is looking for an agreement to make the projects compatible, a rating of −2 is given. Someone who will only agree to the project after being subjected to some form of coercion is rated at −3. Finally, those with a competing project who would rather face the equivalent of death (resign, stay alone, lose part of their salary, etc.) than accept the project are rated −4.

THE SOCIODYNAMIC POSITION OF A PLAYER ALLOWS ONE TO FORECAST REACTIONS TO STIMULI

Equipped with this analysis grid, one can quickly map the positions of the players in relation to the energy they are bringing to the project. Each player receives two marks, one for synergy and the other for antagonism. For example, A might be marked (+3, −2) and B (+2, −3). With practice, it is simple to place each individual on the diagram.

However, the objective is not the drawing of diagrams. The objective is to mobilise the players. As already noted, players other than those who force themselves on the project may be recruited to help ensure its success. Similarly, one must adapt one's attitude to that of the players, depending on their sociodynamic position, in order to improve the chances of the efficient implementation of the strategy.

We will define eight main types of sociodynamic attitudes (see Figure 3.4):

- *The golden triangles*: those in this group have a strong and domineering synergy (+3 or +4) and a certain level of antagonism (−2 or −3). The level of synergy ensures the progress of the project, but there is sufficient antagonism to stand back and to propose improvements. The name is drawn from the triangular grouping in Figure 3.4, and golden refers to their value.
- *The zealots*: a strong synergy for the project and no antagonism. They support the project without question.

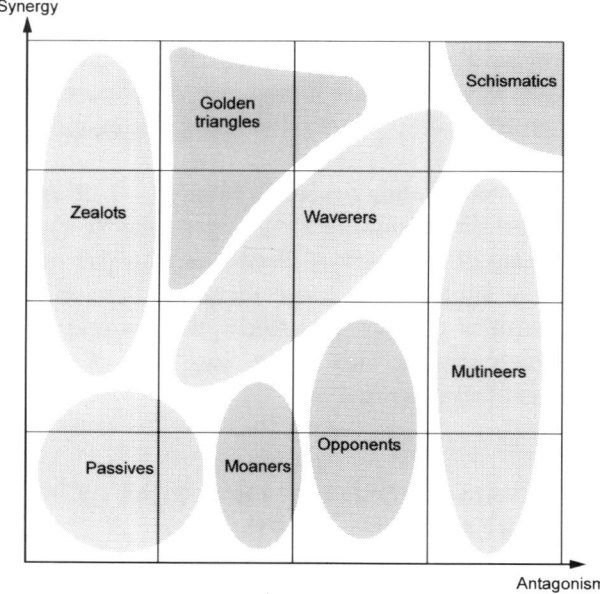

Figure 3.4 The main types of attitudes towards a project

- *The waverers*: these are reasonably involved with a synergy level of +2 or +3. They have an equivalent level of antagonism. This means that, depending on the circumstances, they will or will not support the project. In the diagram, they lie on the 45° diagonal which segments those in favour from those against. By this definition, the waverers are not indecisive. They are, on the contrary, reasonably involved.
- *The passives:* these have weak, or possibly no, synergy or antagonism. The project is not theirs and they have no alternative to offer. The passives are also called 'the silent majority', or more harshly 'the dead weights'. The passives, however, are extremely important for the project because of two characteristics: first, most people fall into this category. Whatever the project the passives represent between 40% and 80% of the players. Second, it is they who will tilt the scales in favour or against the project. The passives are the stakes in the game. If, at the end, they follow the project, then it will be a success. If they follow the opponents, or worse if they do nothing, it will be a failure.
- *The moaners*: these have very weak synergy and little antagonism (−2).
- *The opponents*: the opposite of the zealots, the opponents have more antagonism than synergy. As can be seen, opponents are clearly below the diagonal but they are sensitive to force, unlike the mutineers who are insensitive to everything.
- *The mutineers*: these have very strong antagonism (−4) and weak synergy (+1 or +2). Their antagonism drives them to prefer to lose everything rather than let someone else succeed.
- *The schismatics*: these have the very rare characteristic of high levels of synergy *and* antagonism. The schismatics are, at the same time, totally in favour of the project, but they believe it is not being progressed in the correct manner. They find it difficult to live with this paradox. The perfect example of the schismatic is the entrepreneur who built up a company but is now retired. He keeps his networks operational and is critical of the existing management. However, he is forced to support the firm – as he built it up in the first place – but he hates not being in the driving seat.

With this map, the concept of what is an ally becomes more meaningful:

- The zealots and the golden triangles are allies of *'the first order'*. They will help lead the project.
- The waverers are potential allies and so are *targets* in the campaign.
- The passives are the allies at *stake* in our strategy.

Finally, the sociodynamic map of the project helps develop an implementation strategy which matches the levels of receptivity of each type of player. Each player will react in varying ways to the same stimuli. (These types of behaviour are not personality traits, even if they seem to be. They are types of behaviour regarding a project. The positions so defined do not constitute homogenous groups, but a sum of individuals with different or even opposing expectations. Two golden triangles might well hate each other and be incapable of working together.)

The Golden Triangles

First, it is important to understand that for this type of player a little antagonism is not damaging for the project. A managing director with a dictatorial style will think the opposite; proposals from junior staff to improve the project will be seen as threats from opponents, and the MD will only see the antagonism, not the synergy.

For example, a union representative was described as a notorious opponent simply because she had pointed out certain legitimate salary claims. A further analysis revealed that she had, on her own initiative, stopped a strike by explaining the detrimental effects to the workers — something the management had been unable to do. Still, a robust debate ensued as to whether or not she should be regarded as a golden triangle. A year later she was promoted and the team she managed achieved the best results in the company.

How to Deal with Golden Triangles

First, they must have real concrete responsibilities, that is what they expect. But they have a second role: those outside the project do not see people in the golden triangle as zealots. Waverers respect them for this; and waverers have a key role in persuading the indecisive. Those in the golden triangle can convince waverers because they have an understanding of their concerns, which is not the case with the zealots. Therefore, it is those in the golden triangle who make contact and liaise with the waverers.

Obviously, in exchange, they want an active involvement in the project and to see their ideas come to fruition. Typically they are looking for 'participative projects', such as organising meetings in which they will be the driving force. They should be given these tasks. The problem is in coordinating them, telling them exactly what they can do without going too far. They expect this guidance from the head of the project. They will participate in the steering committees and they will be the spearheads of the project teams.

The Zealots

The opponents call them 'yes men'. They are always in agreement with the head of the project even if they do not fully understand all the issues. Zealots are essential because they raise morale and because they work without being asked to. Even under the fiercest attacks they will continue to fight. They will be at the project leader's side. In the longer term this poses its own dangers as the lack of criticism can lead to mistakes, particularly on attitudes to adopt when dealing with waverers.

There is another limitation: zealots are totally against any compromise. They fail to understand that those who are not totally committed can also enjoy the benefits the project will bring. Only their position is tenable: either you are with them or against them.

At a public meeting on a sensitive project, the company asked one of its managers to make a presentation. He had just completed a similar project on time and to budget – despite an almost impossible deadline. As a favour to his company he had agreed to attend this event. When a local politician asked him a question he exploded with anger as he believed he had already answered it. Somebody was asking stupid questions, that could only be an opponent. When he was quickly replaced he was furious: 'This is a political trap, I am a victim of lazy and untrustworthy politicians who need a scapegoat for their own incompetence'. (And he was right!) These strong feelings are often seen among technical experts who fail to understand the inability of others to see the project as they do.

How to Deal with Zealots

Zealots also have a strong capacity to destroy patiently developed alliances because of their strong extremist attitudes. They are so committed that they refuse to compromise and this can lead to problems in their relationships with the golden triangles.

A recent newspaper article described the relationship between the French and American secret service in the battle against terrorism by extreme Islamic groups. The relationship is typical of one between zealots and golden triangles. The article says:

> When one talks of the French and of terrorism, there is always a certain amount of suspicion from the American side. The two secret services

do not like one another and very rarely work together. The French think that the Americans are like stupid teenagers whose technique is limited to brutal force. The Americans think that the French are devious, ready to mount tortuous operations and to deal with the devil if it is in their immediate interest.

One may recognise the Americans as zealots, who do not like grey areas, and the French as golden triangles, who know how to run with the hare and hunt with the hounds. The tragic aspect of this common situation is that the two sets of allies are working on the same side.

Admittedly, the zealots are the only ones who are totally loyal and can be relied upon with total certainty. Yet, if they cannot be replaced because of their excellent ability to do what is asked of them (only better), it is best if they are excluded from delicate negotiations. Their unswerving support should not lead one to abandon them. Yet, to leave the zealot alone is almost a natural reflex, in which case they often make fools of themselves. Project leaders are generally so busy that they believe they need not spend time with zealots as they are supporting the project anyway. This is a mistake. If the zealots lose their enthusiasm for a project, it will die.

During elections, it is the outsiders from party headquarters who sometimes misjudge the importance of the staunch local allies. Seasoned politicians know their value and how to motivate them. Public meetings, in fact, are held solely for that purpose: they do not win votes, but without the meetings the party faithful feel frustrated, their synergy diminishes and the wind goes out of their sails.

The Waverers

What an unnerving character! The waverer is often referred to in unpleasant, but rarely justified terms, such as time-waster, ditherer, two-faced, and so on. Waverers are important because their doubts strongly reflect the doubts of the passive majority. Although they are less numerous, they have a considerable influence on passives. Allied with the zealots and those in the golden triangle, they can move the project in the right direction.

How to Deal with Waverers

It is clear that the waverers are, after the golden triangles, the second most important grouping. Communicating with them is much easier than communicating with passives, they are at least interested in the subject. Unlike the passives, the waverers read brochures, even if they also read those of the opponents. They ask questions of the company and opponents alike.

Waverers will give their support on certain conditions, and these conditions are signs of synergy on their part. One must listen to them. They form the basis of an agenda for communications and help define those conditions under which they might become more supportive. Waverers are masters of negotiation.

Of course, their support is not of the calibre of the golden triangle. They will say, for example: 'Privately, I agree with you but I cannot say it publicly'. The trick is to find the areas on which they agree to manoeuvre. For example, they offer to organise meetings with certain groups. Good! But these meetings cannot appear to be too much in favour of the project and will an opponent also be invited? Fine, but those promoting the project have conditions too: that the opponent speaks first, that the names of those participating are circulated in advance, and so on.

These 'participative methods' are the ideal tools for waverers. These methods are also used by the golden triangles to air their differences with the project. But, they also have a strong impact on waverers as they allow them to express their reservations. They realise that they are listened to and that their views are taken into account. This will increase their synergy.

The Passives

If the waverers are unnerving, the passives are discouraging. They are intensely disliked by the zealots, but wrongly so. It is also easy to underestimate them. According to Fauvet, it is not the leaders who define the culture and morals of a group, it is the great mass of people who remain unnoticed. It is not the union leader who goes on strike, it is the workers. In the same way, in a company it is neither the boss nor the junior manager who decides if it is normal to arrive on time at meetings. It is the mass of those who, without saying anything, establish a norm and impose their rule on the group. The group then imposes its rule on each individual. Of course the passives do not conceive a change of culture, they follow their leaders, but, in the final analysis, they must ratify any change.

Passives do not like uncertainty. Nor do they like to ask questions because this requires energy and they do not want to spend energy on this project. They like order and simple things. They like the fact that bosses manage the company in such a way as to cause them minimum disruption. They respect the law: not the law written in books or that which has been quickly passed by parliament. No, they respect the law of the group to which they belong, because to break that law requires an energy they do not have.

However, they do not like to be called passives and they do not want to be ignored so that things happen without their knowing. The passives are not simpletons, they are simply not interested. *We are all passive about projects we are not interested in.*

How to Deal with Passives

From all these characteristics one can make some recommendations on how to deal with passives. The most common mistake is asking or forcing them to participate. The passives do not want to waste time. Bosses are there to lead, let them lead. So, they do not like participative methods. One should not force them to voice an opinion or to take a stand as that will probably increase their antagonism.

Even a mailshot can be seen by the passives as a participative action – they have to throw it away! Even this can increase their antagonism. This is a paradox – as passives will make or break the project they must be communicated with, yet any initiative increases their antagonism. So how do we inform them about the project? Passives do not listen to what one tells them. Public meetings? They do not turn up. Local information office? They do not travel. Direct mailing? If it is opened, it is hastily scanned and almost immediately forgotten: it is not their concern. The only way to reach them is through their 'neighbours', be they room mates, office colleagues or next door neighbours. It is essential that the neighbour is an ally of the project.

Passives like being aware of events because, like everyone else, they do not like surprises. Above all, they must have the impression that they have been consulted and that their opinions have been sought. No more is required but they must be involved in the consultation.

They are very concerned that people play by the rules. For example, passives like conflict in debates because they seem fairer. They do not attend of course. But if the project promoters fail to turn up, then they believe there is something to hide unless the passives accept that the debate was fixed or stage-managed by opponents. They dislike events or people who have been manipulated. One must always appear to be 'respectful of rules', even if that seems inappropriate to the situation.

Let's not believe, either, that they do not like the project (or its leaders). No. For them the project promoters are like the opponents – no better, no worse. The essential power of the passives is that of doing nothing. They do not demonstrate, they do not commit themselves, they do not do anything in particular, they do not change. So, one must not depend on strategies which rely on mobilising the passives. They vote because it is part of their 'rules' but they will never go to an election meeting.

The dominating characteristic of the passives is that they will gravitate to the strongest, the one who wins, because this is reassuring. So, first and foremost, one must always appear as the one who represents legitimacy. The position that sways the passives is 'quiet strength'.

The Moaners

The moaners are passives who constantly whinge. They have no synergy, their antagonism is quite moderate and is often limited to spoken words rather than actions. They attend most public meetings, however there is no pleasing them – no matter what is proposed – it is wrong. Their humour is unique and it is generally very sarcastic.

They have little interest or support for the project. Some consider them as opponents who can be tolerated, and through whom one can send messages to true opponents.

How to Deal with the Moaners

Ignore them. Their only use is that they say aloud what many others are whispering. They are an early warning system. They will eventually join the ranks of the passives because they have little energy for the project.

The Opponents

Managers facing difficult situations and strong opposition have a natural tendency to believe that they have been particularly unfortunate to run into one or two strong opponents who have misled all the others. So, in poor neighbourhoods – which are plagued by teenage gangs – the shopkeepers will say: 'These groups are led by a handful of hard core activists; if they could be put in jail, it would be easy to crush the rest, but with the ring-leaders on the loose it cannot be done'. A flurry of accusations aimed at the police follows: 'They do their job but they are too busy and, anyway, the courts release them as soon as they are arrested'.

Their number is always rather vague ('a handful') and the fuzziness of this number is agreed by all the players – be they judges, police, shopkeepers or teachers. This 'handful' is found at all violent protests. But when the leaders are arrested, within a few weeks ten others take their place. It is as if the situation creates – through spontaneous regeneration – leaders who become the spokespersons for these real social tensions, which must be expressed. It is not a good strategy to believe that by getting rid of one person, one gets rid of the problem.

Of course there are always individuals who are naturally bad; but these are generally rejected by society. The power of the opponents is not linked to their personality, but to their ability to exploit real tensions. The only lasting way of eliminating opponents is through their own allies, who would rather have peace and are willing to accept the price.

Opponents can have a synergy of +2 or +1. The former (+2) come to meetings about the project whereas the latter do not even attend. But, globally, the principle is always the same: whether they come or do not come they are not trying to reach an agreement, they have come to explain why they are right and the project is wrong.

How to Deal with Opponents

Opponents are sensitive to strength. This sensitivity is linked to the fact that they still have respect for certain tenets and organisations, for example the law or the company. (One does not immediately see this aspect of opponents.) Trying to identify what they respect is important because it is through this that they can be defeated.

Opponents cannot be convinced, they have to be defeated. How many company directors have been led to believe that they have found a *modus vivendi* or a compromise with an opponent only to find that it turns against them? One can reach an agreement with an opponent as long as one is conscious that the agreement will be repudiated as soon as the respective strengths are reversed.

A client signed an agreement with a strong union after a particularly bad tempered round of negotiations. The client asked: 'Do you believe they will let me work now?' The answer was: 'no'. Two months later, the union came back asking for a general salary raise of 4 per cent for the entire staff, when it had just obtained 6 per cent.

When dealing with opponents the rule is to avoid being kind or looking after interests. The most destabilising attitude to adopt is: 'Why don't you take a running jump'.

The Schismatics

As these are a rather rare breed, let's only touch on them lightly. They are particularly difficult to manage as one can never anticipate their position on a subject. One day it is up, the next day down. Schismatics are pathological cases. It is best not to do anything with them no matter how attractive it might appear. If they turn up, that's fine. If they stay away, that's their problem. Schismatics can expend much energy on the project and they have a phenomenal nuisance power. The only positive point is that they are also a thorn in the sides of opponents who also see them as schismatic.

The Mutineers

There is not much to say about these characters. Not only do they have another project, they have a different view of society. Fortunately these people form only a tiny minority of the population. It is they who assassinate presidents, vandalise machinery during strikes, start fights at public meetings, make nuisance telephone calls in the middle of the night or write hate mail.

How to Deal with Mutineers

The recommendations are the same as for opponents, but never offer a way out. Those who are already in favour of the project, and particularly the passives, would certainly disapprove if this were done. Just as the opponents must be respected for the legitimacy of their opposition, the mutineers must be treated as the danger that they are to society.

POINTS TO REMEMBER

- Sociodynamics measures the energy that a player develops in respect of a project. That energy is twofold: synergy and antagonism.
- The lack of synergy in a player is far more worrying than the level of antagonism.

- Sociodynamics allows one to stipulate and to rate the different types of players who are considered as allies of a project:
    - The zealots and golden triangles are the first-order allies. They are going to lead the project with us.
    - The waverers are potential allies of our actions because they are interested in the project.
    - The passives are the allies that are at stake because it is their support or rejection that will make the decision.
- By using sociodynamic types, one can predict how receptive players will be to differing types of communications:
    - The zealots expect orders, objectives and deadlines, they generally think that participative methods – such as meetings – are a waste of time.
    - The golden triangles and waverers are very sensitive to the information that is given to them, and they like participative methods.
    - The passives are impressionable and follow the crowd. They are not interested in information that is given to them and are resistant to participative methods.
    - The opponents will translate any openness as a weakness or as an attempt to manipulate them.

4 Lateralising the Project

Our definition of allies has a fault: one could be misled into believing that allies are a fixed part of a problem which must be solved. Nothing is further from the truth:

- First, the sociodynamic position of a player is not a fixed part of his or her personality. Depending on the project, the same individual might become a golden triangle, a passive or an opponent.
- Moreover, for the same project that position may vary, depending on time.
- Most importantly, it can vary depending on an individual's understanding of the project.

Crozier explains that a 'player's strategy' (what is called in this book, the 'player's sociodynamic position') depends on two factors: the benefits which are perceived and the constraints. Let's take an example of the constraints which change the player's sociodynamic position.

CASE EXAMPLES

Two Radical Changes of Sociodynamic Positions: The Nimby and the Nimey

There are two acronyms to describe players who suddenly change positions according to place and time: the Nimby and the Nimey. Nimby means 'not in my back yard'. For example, let's suppose a senator from Texas has voted against a new rail line because he associates the car with the concept of freedom and he also supports the development of the oil industry. One day he is told that an oil refinery is to be built in his home town. Suddenly, he turns against the oil industry. This might not be very consistent, but it is understandable. He is a Nimby.

Nimey means: 'not in my election year'. Let's suppose that the senator meets the managing director of the oil company. The latter threatens to cut the financial support he gives to his political party. Then the senator will tell him 'OK, I'll support you. But there is an election coming up. So why not wait until next year to announce your project.' The senator's position might not be very consistent, but he is re-elected. He is a Nimey.

Evaluation

In this single oil refinery project, the position of the senator moves from zealot to opponent, to return to the golden triangle.

The manner is which the project is presented and even the way it is going to develop allows the sociodynamic map to be either improved or worsened. Let's return to the nuclear waste disposal case (see page 8), and see how a project change has fundamentally transformed the sociodynamic map.

Changing the Nuclear Waste Disposal Project

The project objective, as mentioned earlier, is to find a safe underground disposal site for high-level, long-lived radioactive wastes. First, an underground laboratory – in the form of caverns – is planned so that over 15 years the geological and technical conditions at the site can be studied to ascertain its suitability.

Depending on the results of that study, the government will be able to decide:

- whether even more studies are needed;
- whether to build a disposal site in the area; or
- whether to abandon underground disposal altogether.

The project has evolved many times as it has developed. At the start of the project only the underground laboratory was announced, and since it is a geological laboratory it would contain no radioactive material. Initially, the only certainty was the construction of this laboratory. Future disposal or storage of radioactive materials was merely a possibility. This presentation of the project had appealed to the president of the local council. It led to the majority of the council declaring themselves in favour of the laboratory project.

Opponents of the project maintained that the laboratory could be transformed into a disposal facility, in which case there would be radioactive material where the laboratory had been built. Putting the two together, the opponents vociferously claimed that to choose the laboratory was the same as choosing the storage facility. This was a successful strategy for the opponents: presented like this, the project – which had not changed one iota – saw public opinion turn against it; there was now a majority against the laboratory project.

There was no choice but to discuss the possibility of the eventual storage of radioactive wastes. As it turned out, what concerned people was not the storage of these materials but the fact that it was underground. Putting it underground made them suppose that there would be an enormous hole through which the material would be dropped. Then, the hole would be closed up and covered with grass as if nothing had happened. Rumours spread through the community, and the opponents were quick to capitalise on the potential consequences: still-born foetuses, abnormal children and other frightening images.

The authors were asked to mediate and this work consisted mostly of initiating discussions on the conditions under which this storage would be acceptable. It became clear that the key condition was the capability to retrieve the wastes once they had been put underground. If there was a problem, it was argued, then one had to be able to take the wastes out. The company agreed to change the project to include this possibility. The local communities voted in favour of the project, on the condition that retrievable storage would be considered.

Evaluation

The sociodynamic map was shattered by the evolution in the definition of the project. The zealots and opponents did not change their positions at any time. The waverers and passives were the ones who led to the swing in public opinion as a result of their evolving understanding of the project.

This example shows that one way to change the sociodynamic position of a player is to vary the definition of the project.

THE LATERAL PROJECT

A lateral project, is a variation of the original project, which takes into account the views and expressed needs of allies.

This notion originates from the work of Edward de Bono, who developed the concept of 'lateral thinking', a method which allows a debate to take into account the creative contribution of all the participants. De Bono says:

> We can take it that many conflicts are designed by history, by circumstance, by mood and by moment-to-moment developments. We can also take it that many conflicts are designed (not necessarily deliberately) by the parties involved, who focus on differences and crystallize conflict points.

So, de Bono recommends that the positions of the players be 'un-designed'. This is a process which implies disentangling the threads of an argument which have become tangled and confused and to try to reassemble them in another way. He suggests that this be achieved with a method he calls 'lateral thinking'. 'Argument is the most venerated of Western thinking traditions. Much of civilisation is based upon it: for example government and the courts'. He proposes another concept: the constructive thought. This implies that one explores a situation in a constructive way in order to find a solution.

The lateral project may only be one part, or a phase of the original project. Often, the project on which everyone agrees is only one part of the original project. For example, in 1994, the French government preferred not to privatise 100 per cent of the Renault Car Company. It considered that public opinion was ready for the company to be sold, but it was keen to avoid redundancies which might be associated with a complete sell-off.

Similarly, the British Government chose not to privatise all of British Telecom in the mid-80s and by 1993, it was still the biggest shareholder at 22 per cent. This was a reflection of public concern at such an important infrastructure asset being privatised. Although this stake was sold in 1993, the government retained a 'golden share' which gave them powers to block changes in the company's Articles of Association. These were only relinquished in September 1997.

All this might seem obvious. If one's dinner guests refuse dessert because they dislike lemon pie, it is normal they should change their minds if they are suddenly told there is also apple pie. In the real world of

Lateralising the Project

sensitive projects, the practical measures are rarely as simple as changing a dish on a menu. The principle of the lateral project is that the original project can change without changing the benefit that is expected of it. If there is no apple pie, it is probably because the hostess does not like apple pies for it is generally the hostess who bakes. To convince the hostess to change her mind is not a piece of cake! This is the mammoth task which is outlined in detail as the 'strategy of the lateral project' in the second part of this book.

POINTS TO REMEMBER

- A 'lateral project' is a new variation of the original project which will take into account the views and expressed needs of allies.
- The lateral project might only be a part or a phase of the original project.
- One might have to manage several different lateral projects, each adapted to the type of players in order to achieve completion of the project.

5 Identifying Faults in the Players' Behaviour

The quasi-mathematical consideration of the concepts developed in the preceding chapters should not be seen as an underestimation of the very profound nature of sensitive projects. Their management is characterised by its extreme emotional side.

First, it is vital to recognise that there is a key foundation stone for the management of sensitive projects: the behavioural changes which will occur in the players who are under stress. Those who launch a project of Type 2 or 3 are prepared for a bumpy ride. They do not flinch from stormy public meetings, insults to their character, personal attacks, office occupation, physical or psychological threats, all of which are associated with Type 3 projects in particular. During these dreadful moments, some types of behaviour have occurred with such regularity that the authors conclude that they were not simply coincidences, but integral problems which were an essential part of the project and so had to be solved.

Paul Watzlawick, who has written widely on the psychology of communications, says that 'crazy' behaviour is not necessarily the sign of a crazy mind. It might be the only possible response given an absurd and intolerable context. The context of sensitive projects is often absurd and intolerable. Furthermore, the problem won't be solved by choosing people who are immune to these types of behaviour.

Six types of behavioural change have been identified all of which lead to the same result: the diminution of intellectual reasoning and logical argument by allies and opponents and a headlong rush towards violence.

- The *magpie syndrome*. One only sees opponents and ignores one's allies.
- The *avoidance syndrome*. One avoids opponents, that is, practically everyone who is not in total agreement.
- The *stereotype syndrome*. Confronted with individuals one does not know, one categorises them by jumping to conclusions based on stereotypical preconceptions, rather than by trying to have a one-to-one relationship.

- The *frenetic syndrome*. After having once been self-confident, one suddenly panics and starts working like an inexperienced beginner without method, precision or preparation.
- The *paralytic syndrome*. Having received two or three setbacks, one falls into a state of shock – no longer frenetic, even the capacity to think is gone.
- The *'fall guy' syndrome*. In desperation the managers of the project start to criticise one another, rejecting responsibility and apportioning blame to others.

THE MAGPIE SYNDROME

This, the authors believe, is the most common syndrome and paradoxically the least known. Perhaps one goes with the other. The magpie syndrome manifests itself as an obsessive focus on opponents. This focus makes one lose track of essentials, in particular one's allies, and in some cases the objective of the project. This syndrome breeds quasi-obsessional behaviour.

In *Castafiore's Jewels*, the famous Tintin adventure, a magpie, a natural thief, steals the jewels of Captain Haddock's favourite singer, the Castafiore. Everyone is fascinated by the story, but no one questions the behaviour of the bird which is in itself quite surprising. Why should the magpie spend its time stealing shiny objects instead of feeding its chicks by picking seeds and worms as most birds do?

In every sensitive project which the authors have worked on, the same question arises: why is everyone so interested in opponents while showing so little interest in allies – those who advocate and act for the success of the project? Like the magpie, why are people so focused on something or someone in this way? It's the way of the world: when a man is attacked, or faces aggression, he becomes obsessed with his attacker.

An Example of the Magpie Syndrome: The Woodman Case

A service company of 250 people created less than 10 years ago by Mr Woodman is experiencing its first labour problems. The authors are invited in when tension is at its peak. During the first meeting Mr Woodman explains his version of events. In two hours he quotes the names of two union representatives who are leading the conflict 43 times. Not once does he mention the name of a manager. Each episode of his story starts with: '. . . then I tried to do this, and of course the union representatives were against'.

After his explanation was complete, it was proposed that the management team be called together to advise them on action plans. But Mr Woodman says that this cannot be done as the union representatives are going to be against it. We reply: 'That's good, but what do the employees think, what about the other unions?' His immediate response is: 'I do not know, they must be against, they follow the unions!'

Evaluation

This managing director is suffering from the magpie syndrome. Having never experienced a conflict and refusing to accept that there are a few simple problems in the company, he is obsessed by two 25-year-old boys who have taken him for a ride for four months.

As can be seen from this example, the first signs of the magpie syndrome are revealed in the patient's explanations. The second manifestation can be scientifically checked in a very simple way: take a diary and note the following:

- The time spent in the last two months with opponents (for example, negotiating), or preparing actions against the opponents (meetings with lawyers). We will call this number of hours 'h-opponents';
- The time spent with allies to cheer them up, to organise them, to give them help and to stand by them. We will call this number of hours 'h-allies'.

The normal ratio is $\frac{2}{3}$(h-ally) to $\frac{1}{3}$(h-opponent), which implies that one must spend twice as much time with allies as compared to opponents. The reverse relationship reveals a very acute phase of the magpie syndrome.

Following Up the Woodman Case

We analysed with Mr Woodman his diary for the preceding six months. The conflict broke in January following the renewal of some fixed term staff contracts. The absence of a staff representation committee and a demand for subsidised meals only served to increase tensions. We calculated the time spent by Mr Woodman with opponents or because of opponents. We added up the time spent with his lawyers and with union representatives. For good measure, we also added the time spent by the company's managing committees as they also had a role in the conflict.

Then we evaluated the time spent by Mr Woodman with his allies, top management and the staff in general. The ratio showed one hour spent with allies for 20 hours spent with or about opponents.

We finally succeeded in organising a meeting with the management of the company. It was the first such meeting in over three months. The demand from the management is unanimous: 'give us information before you give it to the union representatives. We are finding out from our own workers what your decisions are because they have been told by the union representatives. They are informed and we are not!' It then became clear that the union representatives had demanded that they should be the only channel of information to the workers. The representatives had persuaded Mr Woodman that using his line management to communicate information would increase tension, as workers would see it as being biased. He not only agreed but also accepted that the same information should not be shared with line managers.

Evaluation

Instead of mobilising his allies, Mr Woodman had, consciously or unconsciously, placed his opponents in a highly privileged position. The question he asked us was not: 'how do I get out of this conflict?', or even: 'how do I avoid its recurrence?', but 'how can I get rid of the two union representatives?'. Pointing out the aberrations in his behaviour to Mr Woodman led to a small improvement.

But, in general, the magpie syndrome is stronger than reason. Some managers concentrate all their efforts on only one objective: to respond to the attacks of opponents and to devise ways of making their lives as difficult as possible. They dream about it day and night and think of nothing else. This has some serious consequences.

The magpie syndrome gives too much importance to the opponents. Recently there was a conflict between a local council and some environmentalists on the establishment of a site for highly toxic wastes. The council leader suggested that a debate in the local newspaper on the subject would be a good idea, with two columns for the council and two columns for the environmentalists. That is typical of the magpie syndrome.

At the last elections, the Green Party had only won 7 per cent of the votes, but now they would be, in effect, put on an equal footing with those representatives who had polled more than 90 per cent of the votes. The authors suggested that the six groupings represented on the council should put forward their views, including the environmentalists. In the event, they were the only ones who opposed the project.

The magpie syndrome worries the silent majority. Being preoccupied with opponents has an almost immediate effect: one becomes aggressive, even malicious. Most people try to avoid tension and so will be annoyed at whoever causes it. By paying too much attention to opponents one transforms the debate into a conflict, losing the silent majority – who avoid conflict – on the way.

The magpie syndrome prevents one from addressing allies' concerns and from treating real problems. Paying too much attention to accusations and to the questions of opponents means there is little time to address the concerns of allies. But they too have questions, but generally on other subjects. Being pre-occupied with opponents, allies are ignored. The opponents won't ignore them for very long.

The magpie syndrome hampers one from speaking in a positive and specific way about the project. To respond to attacks is to enter into the world of the opponents' agenda. Even when one responds in a very appropriate manner, one is, in effect, debating the faults of the project. This means the project is not presented in a positive manner, and some projects never get to be presented in a neutral manner to the players concerned. The only depiction of the project that exists is the opponents, and the company's answers to their attacks.

THE AVOIDANCE SYNDROME

This is better known than the magpie syndrome, but it is just as pernicious and is very common. Here, in an unexplainable way, individuals avoid facing any difficult situations. They avoid the topic or, more generally, any occasion to meet the person concerned, and all because of the simple fear of conflict.

For fans of the 'Lucky Luke' comic strip, the avoidance syndrome is better known as the syndrome of the O'Timmins and O'Haras. For five generations, the O'Timmins and the O'Haras have hated one another but they no longer really know why. Yet, when an O'Timmins meets an O'Hara, they do not talk to one another, they shoot. Lucky Luke, the fastest gun in the west, manages through a miracle we will talk about later (the mediation/revelation process) to get the O'Timmins to speak to the O'Haras again. They then become aware that they really didn't hate one another after all; that they had in fact never met.

In sensitive projects adversaries generally have a physical avoidance behaviour towards each other. The only exceptions are the open conflict phases and these battles only feed their desire never to meet. The more tense the situation, the more intense the phenomenon becomes.

An Example of the Avoidance Syndrome: Forecasting Redundancies

A large company is facing a radical change in the work skills needed to run its business. A thorough and expensive review of future employment needs bluntly shows that certain positions will be made redundant in the long term. The results of the review are communicated throughout the company, but the human resources department soon realises that each redundancy seems to come as a complete surprise to each employee. Inevitably, there are heated meetings and widespread unrest and conflict.

On analysis, it becomes clear that the company's managers are fully informed about the redundancy programme. Yet, they never discuss it with the staff who will be affected. As each phase of the programme is finalised and those to be laid off are named, management tells the affected staff: 'The human resources department would like to see you'. Those being made redundant learn from the person in charge of training, what their boss has known for two years: that the position is redundant.

This is classical 'hot potato' management – throwing the problem to human resources by saying: 'we are technical managers, we are only in charge of technical matters. You are the human resources director so take care of human resources'. The management is, in fact, helped by the staff themselves who have absolutely no desire to confront the problem that they suspect exists.

Evaluation

This is the classical avoidance syndrome. The management avoids the issue of the professional future of an employee, because it knows that the meeting could lead to conflict and be painful. Once this avoidance phenomenon was identified, it was easy to introduce a system of career meetings, with a step-by-step follow up by the management. Obliged to face reality, the management and the employees concerned were able to find individual solutions for over half the cases. The last phase of the redundancy programme took place without any conflict.

What is the cause of avoidance syndrome? It's as if every event seems designed to induce behaviours that systematically increase the distance from the real or supposed opponent. (Unlike 'ostrich politics', which is merely a lack of courage, the avoidance syndrome is unconscious.) Many people have a pathological relationship to conflict, they would rather do anything than get into an acrimonious situation. When one does want to get into contact, one is confronted with the same difficulty: the other party is affected by the same syndrome and also refuses any contact.

Most individuals seek to create a world that resembles them, which corresponds to what they know. They generally meet only those individuals whose judgement they can anticipate – similar to their own, of course. Consequently they will avoid facing people who might possibly shatter their perceptions of the world. In a sensitive project only the most aggressive opponents come into contact, and then it is with the purpose of creating conflict. The others, the passives and the waverers do not even listen. The effort to make contact has to originate from allies of the project.

One of the principles of modern diplomacy is never to leave a country with which one has diplomatic difficulties. France didn't close its embassy in Libya when there were difficulties there. This principle not only helps protect future markets, but its most important function is to keep a line of communication open with whoever one is in conflict with. The bad old days, when countries closed their embassies at the least hint of a diplomatic incident, are gone.

The avoidance syndrome has a number of characteristics:

- It favours the accumulation of problems and so is self-perpetuating: the less adversaries see of each other, the more problems build up. As more problems build up, more misunderstandings arise. With more and more misunderstandings, the prospects of a meeting become infinitesimal.
- It favours a lack of understanding of the other's position: since one does not meet the other person, one cannot know what he or she really thinks. One is led to make sense of events from far away and to rely on so-called 'well-informed' people.
- It favours extremists and liars since there is no-one to contradict their interpretations of the position of the other person.

THE STEREOTYPE SYNDROME

The stereotype syndrome first strikes those who are unsure of their ground. In the field of sensitive projects, the syndrome affects many people. Those who suffer from this syndrome fail to see people as individuals but tend to bunch them into homogenous groups which are then given stereotypical qualities.

Let's take a manager who has never done any business with the media. Generally, it is the role of the public relations department. But suddenly his project is in the news and he has to face the local newspaper. He has only heard terrifying stories about the media: how the facts are twisted; people are quoted out of context; they are biased in favour of the environmentalists and the like. He has become the victim of his own prejudice: he is going to meet *the* media, he is going to hate *the* media, he is going to prepare 'something to say to *the* media' as if '*the media*' was not a group of individuals with diverse expectations and characteristics, but a homogenous and somewhat diabolical group.

Certainly, it is simpler and quicker to sort people into categories than to try to know them as individuals. With sensitive projects one is facing people that are difficult to understand and one does not know them as individuals, be they lawyers, trades unionists, politicians, ministers, directors or journalists. Then, one advances by hearsay which means that one starts with preconceived ideas.

> **An Example of the Stereotype Syndrome: The Disposal Case**
>
> A project to establish a disposal site for highly toxic wastes is not going well. The whole region seems to be on the verge of turmoil, and the authors are called when tensions are highest. As part of the mediation work we meet a senator from the socialist party. His analysis of the situation is quite simple: 'You should know that this project is going to be approved without any problems' he says. 'The council is dominated by a right wing coalition and so, it votes for the government policy. We socialists will support it because we are in favour of science. Against it, there will only be the hard left and you know they hold only a few seats on the council'.
>
> The authors then went around the county, met over 150 people – some in favour of the project and some against. One fact became patently clear: there was no link between support or opposition for the project and political allegiance. The leaders of the group that had been formed to fight the waste disposal site included a right wing politician, a communist, an environmentalist and two people who were not members of any political party.
>
> **Evaluation**
>
> Our politician is suffering from an advanced case of the stereotype syndrome. For him, life is organised into political families and there are only four types: conservatives, centrists, socialists and the hard left. This simple categorisation may work in the cosy atmosphere of the parliament, but it has drawn him apart from realities on the ground. In fact he was badly damaged politically because of the position he took on the waste disposal site.

Whether one is dealing with company rescues, large infrastructure projects or important political reforms, one meets very clever and fine analysts who reduce the problems of the opposition to two or three hackneyed phrases. These are supposedly an explanation of why things are going wrong.

The key characteristic of the stereotype syndrome is the *globalisation of behaviours*. When the leader of a project or the members of his team say: 'The supervisors are against this' or 'Everyone is on strike', it is because they have this tendency to fall into the trap of the stereotype syndrome. Experience shows that these broad generalisations are almost always false. Some meetings on the ground will show that there is possibly a majority of the supervisors against something, but it is not all the supervisors and their opposition is focused on some particular aspects of the project, which may have been badly presented or certainly badly understood.

The stereotype syndrome is very serious for two reasons:

- First, it leads one to misunderstand the situation. For example, to think that supervisors are against the project can lead one to bypass them in the implementation plans. This will certainly have a negative effect.
- Second, and most important, it leads to self-filling prophecies. Everyone knows that our attitude influences the attitude of others towards us; to assume that all the supervisors are not reliable can force one to adopt an attitude which is going to shock them and consequently make them unreliable.

In a recent case of industrial unrest, two of the 23 supervisors were leaking information to the unions. The top management decided to stop briefing the supervisors instead of facing the two people concerned. The supervisors concluded that the management was not taking them seriously and adopted a wait-and-see policy which bordered on the hostile.

THE FRENETIC SYNDROME

The frenetic syndrome manifests itself when an individual has to make hasty, numerous and contradictory decisions as a result, generally, of being overpowered by time, by fear or by the excitement of a crisis.

In those projects that have really gone astray, one meets many managers who, at the end, say: 'how could I have been so stupid!' Their remark is often touching – powerful people, they normally draw up careful strategies and tactics before launching their campaigns. However strong opponents and the avoidance syndrome lead them to forget to take the appropriate amount of time to analyse the problems. This has two consequences:

- *Everyone gathers around the decision-maker*. Those who in normal times bring a healthy amount of criticism to the decision-making process display the symptoms that have just been described.
- *Time is too short* to analyse the problems with the appropriate amount of attention.

Then, all actions are taken as if the decision-maker were trapped in a cul-de-sac. Every exit door is tried individually, even when they seem improbable. The legendary lucidity disappears. In fact a boss who harshly punishes an employee on strike (tension strategy), and who sees the conflict spread as a result of the decision, will often suggest a settlement where everything is conceded!

An Example of the Frenetic Syndrome

A company introduces changes in its method of payment of staff from weekly to monthly. After two months there is uproar following some recurring salary mistakes. Following the tensions created by these mistakes the unions assemble a much larger list of demands including salary rises. For some unexplained reason the mistakes keep on cropping up for another four months, leading to a number of work stoppages. These conflicts force the company to give in on quite a few of the unions' demands.

An analysis reveals that the measures to correct the salary system had already been taken in the first month. But these measures had been taken hastily without consulting the person in charge of the department, who was considered not very competent. There was no preparation for the changes and no follow-up. So, these measures were not enough to correct the system fully. The following month other measures, also badly prepared, superseded the first. This created even more trouble. In six months, six series of measures, all contradicting each other, were put in place. In the end the person in charge of salaries did not know which rules were in use.

Evaluation

This classic case of the frenetic syndrome features a meddlesome boss who is trying to do good. Instead of trusting the system he himself has implemented, he prefers to do everything himself and in great haste. The first measures taken were good ones. It would have been enough to explain them and to follow through their implementation. But he continued to meddle. He was too destabilised in his role as the all-seeing boss to do it any other way.

It is always startling to witness the amazing difference between the frenzied activity of the management team caught up in the excitement of the frenetic syndrome, and the almost total lack of action among those on the shopfloor or on the ground. The succession of orders and counter-order leads, in effect, to nothing happening.

The frenetic syndrome has three consequences:

- It leads to the *wrong decisions being made* which take care of the immediate problem but which pose a threat to the future success of the company.
- It leads to some *good decisions with such tight deadlines that they become totally impossible to understand and impossible to implement* and so become a source of tension.
- It *destabilises the management systems*, which are the lifeblood of the company, at the very moment when these systems are essential to implement the change.

THE PARALYTIC SYNDROME

The paralytic syndrome manifests itself when an individual is so panicked that decisions are not taken. This syndrome is at the same time the opposite and a parallel counterpart of the frenetic syndrome. When one is in a state of frenzy, others react by being paralysed. The most surprising thing is that this paralysis does not just affect the project but also all the other issues being handled by the project manager.

In tense situations, what causes the most damage is not making mistakes but doing nothing at all. With the paralytic syndrome the person in charge rejects all proposals to solve a problem. Only the downside is seen and the benefits of a decision are ignored.

Conflict is often compared to a game of chess, where every move is made according to a strategy which should lead to the opponent's defeat. But life is different to chess – one can make many moves while the opponent is considering the position. To make good moves is certainly important, one should not move foolishly, but would raw beginners be able to beat grand masters if they could make ten times as many moves? Perhaps the game 'go' is a better analogy in that its proposition is: whoever exists more than the other eventually wins.

There are two causes of the paralytic syndrome: fear and tiredness. Difficult projects test the nerves of the decisions-makers. They can burn out. One has only to look at the physical state of a manager who loses, one by one, all of those things in life which were considered safe and certain, especially if these beliefs were strong and deeply seated. Paralysis often follows from frenzy: the manager has played too many careless moves with disastrous consequences. Thus, the fear to move will slowly emerge: like the punch-drunk boxer who pushes his seconds away.

For example, a managing director postpones for as long as possible the presentation he must give to the sales force because it might not be a pleasant experience, as the company is not doing well. Every decision is so carefully analysed and discussed that meetings follow meetings and nothing ever happens. So, the paralytic syndrome is the last stage of a doomed project which occurs just before the final failure. Everyone is ready to throw in the towel.

THE FALL GUY SYNDROME

Individuals suffering from the 'fall guy' syndrome are not trying to solve problems, they are looking for those responsible – 'those who made the mistakes'. They do not act, they punish. They are not looking for solutions, they are looking for guilty parties.

At a higher level, the 'fall guy' syndrome becomes collective: every member of the team accuses someone else for the failure. Sufferers of the syndrome systematically criticise the behaviour of the other players, particularly that of allies. This is the ultimate symptom that the project has gone off the rails: the allies of the project are not just finding fault with the opponents, they are criticising their own camp.

Two phenomena will then be observed:

- First, the 'fall guy' will be used more often. From everywhere and everyone, criticisms are bursting forth. Those who are criticised are, in return, criticising those who criticised them. Followers of transactional analysis would say that the 'score cards' are about to be used. All the micro-tensions which had been buried will surface. Earlier agreements, where partners had agreed a compromise, are about to reappear as the obvious reasons for failure: a key appointment was a mistake, the wrong sector was chosen, there was not enough market research. Everyone is distancing themselves from the others and from the project in general.
- Second, whoever is in charge of the project becomes the favourite target of criticism.

In the final phase, the 'fall guy' syndrome becomes the scapegoat syndrome. A player is accused of all the mistakes and everybody agrees to blame that player for everything that went wrong. Most of the time, it is the project leader. René Girard, the renowned French philosopher, shows that the scapegoat is usually the person, who was the most highly regarded, and took the greatest care in making decisions.

This phenomenon is not necessarily a bad thing for the project: of course it is a horrendous experience for the victim. But, in fact, this can be a protective reaction from society, as René Girard brilliantly demonstrated. Badly managed, it leads to the dismissal of the person and team responsible and the project is stopped – generally for a very long time. Well-managed, the scapegoat syndrome can help the project resume afresh and on solid ground as the person responsible for all the mistakes has been sacrificed. Nasser, after the failure of the Six-Day war, succeeded with this clever trick.

Some management gurus believe that for revolutions to be successful, there must be a number of stages: a true revolution requires a series of leaders to be wasted on a project for the final leader to succeed. It is the ultimate leader who seems to be the only efficient one. However, all the predecessors made it possible.

In those troubled times where a project is under threat, one likes to imagine that one would act like Bonaparte on the Arcole Bridge on 15 November 1796. The future emperor sees the enemy forcing his troops to retreat from the not yet famous bridge. He takes a flag from the hands of a corporal hit by enemy fire and throws himself towards the enemy, leading foot soldiers who have been inspired by his courage.

Not everybody is Bonaparte and not everybody is as lucky. Certainly, courage is a necessary attribute when managing sensitive projects, but one has to be cautious not to derive it from just one person since that courageous person would make an ideal scapegoat in the event of failure.

When forced to retreat, it is generally best patiently to seek reinforcements in the form of allies before leading the next assault. This is less stylish but more efficient and long-lasting. Paradoxically, the greater the apparent strength of a leader, when things turn sour the weaker he or she will appear. On the contrary, whoever seems involved in complicated games or alliances will more easily emerge from the crisis.

POINTS TO REMEMBER

- The reasons for sensitive projects going astray are not just associated with organisational problems, they are also due to the defensive reactions of the players under stress.
- It is not only by precise procedures, by coordinating meetings or by having a close follow-up of the project that one can stop the project going astray.
- The context of sensitive projects is often absurd and hard to live with. Choosing people who can resist stress won't, in itself, be sufficient to manage a sensitive project.
- In order to stop the project going astray, players must be equipped with tools which enable them to understand what is happening and which provide them with a reassuring 'helping' hand at their side.

Part II
Launching the Project

In the first part of this book some landmarks have been established which help guide the way within sensitive projects. The importance of segmenting the field of play and analysing the sociodynamics of the players were emphasised. These landmarks are extremely useful as will be seen, but the real challenge is putting this into action.

What to do, and when to do it, when nothing is simple? And once the decision is taken, how can the project be brought to a successful conclusion without stumbling along the way? Experience of sensitive projects reveals that decision-makers often have the same fears as the ageing boxer who has been hit once too often. Even the smallest initiative meets a mountain of preconceptions and criticisms because there is no longer the will to keep going. The first move, and every subsequent move causes a great deal of pain, aggression and resistance. Each player, and possibly even the leader of the project, feels like a trench soldier in the First World War destined to be sacrificed merely to gain a few centimetres of ground.

A normal project is, in many ways, like 'well-mannered' games such as chess. Here, the player who wins the white pieces has the advantage of making the first move and is pleased with this advantage. A sensitive project is more like 'bad tempered' full contact sports such as karate. Here, the fighting is real. Whoever strikes first is also taking the risk of lowering his or her guard and thus receiving a blow. One never knows if this is going to be the 'knock-out' blow. The referee must often threaten to penalise the competitors for not fighting because both refuse to initiate an attack. The first strike is therefore difficult. So how should the project be launched?

In Chapter 6, some strategies, which are bad, are considered and discarded. In Chapter 7, the principles of a strategy more suitable to sensitive projects are examined – this is the strategy of the lateral project. Chapter 8 looks at the first moves – the steps towards mediation–revelation.

6 Strategies that Do Not Work

For a project here are four strategies which can be implemented which do not work. There are two 'classical' strategies which have, on many occasions, been shown to be futile. These are the Samurai strategy and the Participative strategy. Two other strategies originate from a misinterpretation of sociodynamics: the Noah's Ark strategy and the Machiavelli strategy. These strategies are reviewed (but forewarned is forearmed!).

THE SAMURAI STRATEGY – TOO HARSH

The Samurai strategy consists of launching a project as if nothing else mattered: it either makes or breaks. 'But, come on, Mr Smith, go ahead, what are you waiting for?' is the classical sentence that one hears in companies. For the civil servant it is something like: 'the minister is particularly keen for this project to be implemented quickly'. Sometimes it works, in which case it really was not a sensitive project. On most occasions the project fails. Then there are two ways out: conflictual and non-conflictual.

The Conflictual Way Out

The project is launched and the opponents are shocked and horrified, they alert the waverers who then warn the passives. Tension rises. The decision-makers are angry and are demanding results, they talk of sanctions. Tension rises higher still, the field of play becomes a battle ground with open conflict. The decision-makers, suddenly afraid, retreat and propose arbitration. Generally they go behind the back of the project leader, who is disowned. The peace-keeping army settles in. One gets then to the second stage of the strategy after having lost three months and a significant sum of money.

The Non-Conflictual Way Out

This is seen more frequently in times of crisis. The opponents are not up in arms; they are too afraid, for example, of losing their jobs. They undermine the project, consciously or not, through sabotage. For example, there was a breakdown in the telecommunications network in a large firm. Work came to a halt. Yet, everyone refused to reset the 'router' (a simple push of a button) to make the network operational because everyone was 'afraid of doing something silly'. The cumulative effect of such micro-incidents is enough to kill projects, much more certainly than a good conflict which is visible and which can be fought.

Technical problems, not human problems, are seen as the reason for the setback. There is the real risk that substantial amounts of time and money will be spent on trying to solve technicalities, which are not the real problems. The human tensions, however, are very real and are unlikely to disappear. Certainly, it is easier to challenge technical questions than to manage social issues.

The Samurai strategy has three faults: it discourages allies who believe they are not listened to; it gives too much weight to opponents; and, most of all, it stops the project being considered again for a long time. For example, when some banks found themselves lagging behind the competition with outdated computer systems, they faced problems introducing a new one. A previous project which was ill-prepared is used by the opponents as a scarecrow. This scarecrow is waved by the opponents and it frightens everyone each time any new computer project is suggested.

So what of the Samurai strategy? Whether it be evolutions in society or the increased wisdom of decision-makers, it is no longer in fashion.

PARTICIPATIVE STRATEGY – TOO WEAK

The second classical method of implementing a project is the Participative strategy. It starts from the principle that, by linking people to a change, one lowers the risk of them taking a stand against the project. The strategy involves the launching of a vast consultation exercise based on work-groups and meetings in order to prepare opinion and 'to work together to make the project happen'.

In theory it is a more delicate strategy than the Samurai strategy, but in practice it achieves the same result: the project does not come to a brutal end, it sinks in quicksand.

The Case of the Bank

A large banking group – reacting to increased competition in the marketplace – wants to change the work conditions of its employees, mainly to increase opening hours and to introduce multiskilling. The managing director, knowing how sensitive staff are about maintaining benefits they have acquired over the years, launches a company-wide review on the theme of 'tomorrow's skills'.

A few months are lost with discussions on the best way to organise the consultation. Finally, some groups manage to get together. They grasp the fact that the project difficulties are nothing compared to the numerous human relations problems threatening the bank. These groups throw themselves into a deep analysis of the cause of these difficulties. It appears, in fact, that all of these must be treated before any other action can be initiated. Finally, not a single action materialises. Two years later, the chief executive is dismissed.

Evaluation

As predicted by sociodynamics, opponents took advantage of the forum that was offered to them. The zealots did not participate because they thought that 'participative methods' were a waste of time. The golden triangles were discouraged when they saw the length of the process and the weak outcome.

To adopt the participative method with numerous opponents has two unfortunate consequences:

- It gives the strongest opponents a forum to speak out.
- It overloads the project with problems that are not its own. To start a project with the condition that all existing problems must be solved postpones any change.

The participative strategy is the right one to adopt when:

- globally, the players have more synergy than antagonism; and
- there are micro-tensions and local adaptations to be made.

Therefore, the participative strategy is perfectly suited to:

- 'normal' projects. . .
- . . . that have a long time-scale.

However, for a sensitive project where players with bad faith abound, where opponents are determined and discussions rather complex, the participative strategy is unsuitable. Its only possible merit is to give time to time. It suits those managers who know that their days are numbered so they stay clear of the poison chalice that was neatly planned for them.

NOAH'S ARK STRATEGY – CLEVER BUT USELESS

To the gifted amateurs of sociodynamics, it is immediately obvious that the above two classical strategies do not take into account the behaviour of the players. One must favour those who have the most synergy – allies – this is the principle of the allies' strategy.

One must find a way of getting only allies to participate in the project, to list them, get them together, organise them, separate them from the rest of the world. This is the Noah's Ark strategy. After the deluge, Noah wanted the world to begin anew on a sound footing. He chose good people to join him on the Ark and left the others to drown. As we see today from the world around us, Noah's strategy did not deliver the expected results. One example of this type of strategy became famous: that of the Saturn project.

A Noah's Ark Strategy: The Saturn Project

At the beginning of the 1980s General Motors had to face fierce competition from the Japanese in its domestic US market. After attacking and gaining a significant share of the small-car market, the Japanese began to achieve considerable success with the sales of their medium and large cars.

The head of General Motors, Robert Stempel, had tried almost everything to improve the productivity of his company. He decided to show the rest of the world that Americans were capable of making a reasonably priced car which was as good as anything produced by the Japanese.

He created a new company – the Saturn Corporation. This was a remarkable decision as General Motors already had the greatest number of known car brands in the world (Chevrolet, Cadillac,

Plymouth, Pontiac, Buick). He put together a special team, drawn from the best employees from within and outside General Motors. At the same time the company was laying off tens of thousands of employees. A special factory at Spring Hill, Tennessee was constructed at the same time as a dozen others were closed, particularly in Detroit, Michigan. From scratch, a dealer network was created using the best of GM's and others' sales forces.

The first Saturn car rolled off the production lines in November 1990. In January 1991, the factory produced 1520 cars a month, in January 1992, 16 757 a month and in July 1992, 22 305. By 1993, Chevrolet dealers watched as stocks piled up on their forecourts while customers had to wait six weeks for the basic Saturn model. The Saturn project was a success. Meantime, dealers of other GM brands began to go into bankruptcy through lack of sales.

Unfortunately, General Motors' results did not improve as a consequence. On the contrary, it was as if the energy spent on creating Saturn had been drained from the main company. And Saturn's results didn't make up for the losses of other brands. Robert Stempel wanted to show that he was not a bad boss, that it was the company which was bad. In fact, he showed that it is easier to create a new company rather than renew an old one.

Evaluation

What is a good worker, what is a good dealer, if not an ally? Stempel had, in fact, implemented an allies' strategy: he, purely and simply, eliminated passives, waverers and opponents. Not surprisingly, by acting this way, his project turned out to be a success. The problem was that he didn't reach his main and first objective: to increase GM's profits.

The Noah's Ark strategy maintains that one should do what is feasible, with those who are in agreement. But, first, the objective is not to have one's allies change, it is to have the allies change everyone else and, second, one does not often have the possibility of dealing only with allies. Most of the time we must also contend with passives and opponents. Therefore, the Noah's Ark strategy is not suitable for sensitive projects.

MACHIAVELLI'S STRATEGY – INVALID BY ITS VERY PRINCIPLE

The other possible approach consists of working as a secret society. As with Machiavelli, this involves identifying one's allies, weaving a network around them like a spider's web at which one is at the centre. From here one controls an invisible little world.

In many firms, some very famous, this type of strategy is used. Relationships are created between dynamic individuals on specific strategic options. The ideological fights are happening but in the silence of the boardrooms. The project never appears in the light of day.

With experience one realises that this is not what makes companies progress. Machiavelli's strategy creates within an organisation deep-seated opposing clans. It raises the power of whoever is most active by highlighting the difference between those 'in the know' and the others. However, it comforts the passives in their role as passives.

As noted in the first part of this book, the objective in a sensitive project is to create a collective dynamic which includes the passives, who are the 'stakes' being played for. At some stage or other this dynamic must go through a collective process which is not possible with Machiavelli's strategy. Common sense would dictate that if there is no opportunity to have an agreement, there cannot be an agreement. However, there can't be a solid agreement without, at some stage, a collective process. Machiavelli's strategy is not a strategy for change, it is a power strategy. Its objective is not the organisation's progress, but the advancement of some people within it.

Projects are characterised by key moments: the moment when the project is disclosed to the group and when the group takes ownership of it. For that dynamic in favour of a project to appear, one needs:

- that at that precise moment one is capable of bringing together a group of potential allies who represent the field of play, and that collectively they form a team to lead the project; and
- that this core team has only one dynamic, to conquer all the players around the project.

To organise this delicate path between the decision to launch a project and the time when a group of allies is going to take charge of it, the 'herdsman strategy', which is described in the next chapter, is recommended.

POINTS TO REMEMBER

- The Samurai strategy has three faults: it discourages allies who do not feel they are listened to, it gives too much power to opponents and, when it fails, it stops the project for a long time.
- The Participative strategy is suitable for 'normal' projects . . . which have a long time scale.
- Noah's Ark strategy pretends to do what is do-able with those who agree, yet:
  - the objective is not to change one's allies, but to get the allies to make others change;
  - moreover, one does not often have the possibility of dealing only with allies. Most of the time one must contend with passives and opponents as well.
- Machiavelli's strategy leads to the formation of deep-seated opposing clans.

To create a dynamic for a project, the strategy must:

- come from a hard core of allies representing the field of play;
- motivate this hard core to have one dynamic only – to conquer all the other players around the project.

7 The Strategy of the Lateral Project

The last chapter stated that a good strategy must take into account the necessity to make players act in a dynamic way. But what is a player's dynamic? Almost every managing director has said: 'Today, I will do nothing and let's see if the place continues to run smoothly'. As a matter of fact, life continues as normal. It is as if a collective energy allowed events to happen without the need to ask for them to happen or without the need for anyone to instigate them.

SENSITIVE PROJECTS

In a sensitive project, this focusing of the collective energy of the players does not exist. At best it is dissipated over a multitude of other projects, at worst it is focused against the project. It is then that one begins to perceive that collective energy is an illusion: there is only the sum of individual energies. The leaders of many sensitive projects could learn much from the strategies derived from the humble herdsman.

A Sensitive Project: Crossing the River

The herdsman often needs to move his cattle across a river. The animals do not like this as they are fearful of the water. Unlike the scenes in western films he does not start shooting in the air as this would scare the beasts and – working alone – he would have an impossible task to get them all back together. Nor does he whip the most stubborn who have stopped to graze. Cows are touchy creatures and are quite capable of lashing out and injuring him.

The herdsman thus starts by searching for Buttercup, Daisy, Nellie and Baby Eyes because he knows that he can count on them. He calmly puts a bell around their necks and then he leads them to the river. Cows – being sociable creatures – will instinctively follow this sudden move. Without having been given any orders, Buttercup, Daisy *et al.* take most of the cattle to the opposite side and the herdsman has time to round up the laggards.

Evaluation

It must be stressed that people are not cows – nor is it suggested that they should be treated as such. However, within the herdsman strategy there is an inborn respect for many of the principles that should be adopted for sensitive projects.

1. First, *the herdsman does not consider his cattle as a static object but as a dynamic entity.* What he notices at a glance is the energy emanating from the cattle. He is not going to move them if they are grazing. He waits until the cattle have finished with one patch of ground and hunger pangs encourage the herd to move to a new pasture.
2. Moreover, *he doesn't see a herd of cattle but a sum of individuals.* This results in a collective energy.
3. *He identifies allies and organises them so that their move generates a collective move.* In a sensitive project, one must start to work with the players who are in favour of the project. But it is not enough to identify them. There is also the need to organise them so that they can act together. The leaders of the cattle were already allies before the bell was put around their necks. What made the movement of the cattle possible was not to have identified them as allies, it was to get them to act together.
4. *He waits for the allies to obtain the expected result,* maybe by helping them with a few encouraging sounds but no more.
5. Finally, once the allies have done most of the work and brought with them most of the passives, he takes care of the laggards. These will begin to feel isolated on the other bank and will hurry to rejoin the rest of the herd.

The Strategy of the Lateral Project

The actions to be taken by the leader of a sensitive project can be directly linked to the herdsman strategy:

- Identify potential allies.
- Mobilise them.
- Give them the means of persuasion and, above all, have confidence in them to find the right way.
- Then there will be time to take care of the stubborn ones.

Obviously, such an approach is a little disconcerting when one is leading an information technology project to computerise the sales force: one cannot choose some people and leave the others behind. What appears right for the cattle seems out of place for administrative assistants in a large organisation. In this case it is easy to believe it must be everyone or no one. It is difficult to see oneself explaining to the managing director that one is only dealing with those employees who are ready to accept change, and it is slightly alarming to think that administrative assistants would refuse to obey orders.

In fact, this is exactly what happens. Even if they are employees and they are paid to do the job – they may well refuse to do what is asked of them. Which is exactly why this book has been written! Experience shows that if the administrative assistants are highly unionised and are in the habit of going on strike over trivial matters, it will seem normal to 'phase in' the project. For example, one could start with pilot groups or by refurbishing the work area so that the pilot teams can organise themselves differently.

Step by step, and after long negotiations, the new operation is spread to the rest of the group, possibly leaving out the oldest who would be given the choice of remaining with the old system while waiting for retirement. The situation is exacerbated when the players in a project have no dependence on the project leader, as is the case with elected representatives, communities and local associations.

ONLY THE ENERGY OF ORGANISED PLAYERS COUNTS

Let's, however, go a bit further in the analysis of sociodynamics, and also note two facts:

- First, as previously seen, the players of a project are not just set in stone but, to a certain extent, are the consequences of a strategy.
- Second, and this will be examined in detail later, the energy which allows a project to succeed is not the sum of individual energies, but only the sum of the energies of the players who have managed to act together.

If one was to undertake a survey among the cattle before launching the 'crossing the river' project, it is very unlikely there would have been a majority in favour. Individuals normally do not like change. Yet the cattle decided to follow and they were quite happy since the grass was more luscious on the other side of the river. But at the start of the project, there was only a minority of allies. However, they were the ones who finally created the 'social dynamism' of the cattle. What creates this social dynamism (which dictates the success or failure of a project) is the capacity of the players, whether in favour or against, to organise themselves and to convey this organisation to the rest.

The herdsman had opponents. They might even have been more numerous than his allies. But his opponents were less well-organised than his allies. This explains why certain projects, even though supported by only a minority succeed: the players in favour have a level of organisation superior to the players against.

And so the death penalty is abolished in France and Great Britain when all the opinion polls show that a majority are in favour. There are more allies for the project 'in favour of the death penalty', but the allies of the project 'for the abolition of the death penalty' are better organised (even if they are also extremely diverse and there is more than one grouping of them).

Since collective energy is the sum of the energy of the organised players, then the objective for whoever is behind a sensitive project, consists of helping the players in favour of the project to organise themselves. For example, in the case of the Newbury by-pass the energy should have been developed not to fight the tree-dwelling activists, but to organise those local people, and those in Portsmouth and Southampton, who will work for the project.

The Strategy of the Lateral Project

What is meant by the strategy of the lateral project is the development of energy with the goal and with the effect of placing allies in a situation from which they can support the project, so that at the same time they can:

- individually dedicate more energy to the project, or use this energy for actions that favour the project;
- manage to organise themselves so that the effects of their actions multiply and spread to the players who are still only spectators.

That might mean:

- encouraging them to form a support committee;
- encouraging them to create a study group; or
- encouraging them to launch a pilot scheme in their sector, etc.

In summary, this means *the allies must be made to act and their contribution must be a collective one*. Of course allies, apart from 'zealots', will have their own game plans, so that their actions will bring personal benefits. But that matters little if their actions contribute to the success of the project.

An Individual Action for a Project: Reform of the Dockers' Status

In many countries, dockers have enjoyed special benefits and the project to reform their status has led to bitter and long drawn out strikes. During one action, a major shipping magnate issued a press release warning that he was about to change to another harbour if the strikes continued. This decision was, of course, very much in his own interest. But it was also a positive action for the ongoing reforms. This 'ally' was asked to warn the other players of his impending action and to be sufficiently loud to attract the media. Quite often, one notices that the ally is ready to act but simply doesn't know what to do. And neither do the project managers.

Evaluation

This action was helpful but was not as efficient as a collective action. If, on the same day, all the tanker owners had made a joint statement threatening to boycott the harbour, the effect would not only have been multiplied, it would have been more long-lasting.

IT IS MUCH EASIER TO ENCOURAGE ALLIES TO ORGANISE THEMSELVES FOR THEIR OWN PROJECT – A LATERAL PROJECT

Let's be precise: to 'organise oneself' does not mean to 'organise'. To organise is to tell people what is the norm, what procedure to follow, what steps to take, how the job is going to be done. Organising players is the role of the leader of a normal project.

In sensitive projects, the players don't accept the norm or the organisation that one is trying to impose on them. So we can define the objective of the lateral project strategy as: *to discover together* the norm, the processes, and the way to act which will lead a certain number of players to work concurrently for the project, whereas they didn't do so beforehand.

A Lateral Project for Productivity Gains: The Case of Factory 2000

An international group buys a textile company. After a structures audit it is decided to introduce a new production process in the main factory, but all change is resisted. Seen from the head office of the international group this is a straightforward project to increase productivity. Seen from the factory the project is impossible. Therefore the team will start by looking for members of middle management who are mostly in favour of the change. It will organise with these small groups a series of brain-storming meetings on the changes. From this, a project develops which will include elements leading to an increase in productivity, but which will also improve working conditions and skills. This new project, which the authors call 'the lateral project', will be retitled 'the factory 2000 project', which is substantially more far-reaching than a mere productivity project. Presented this way, it is much more likely to win the support of the majority of the employees. In fact, it has become a project of the training department and so the factory 2000 project will perform well above expectations.

Evaluation

As originally presented by the new owner, the project would have undoubtedly led to conflict which in turn could have led to the closure of the factory. The way the nuts and bolts of a lateral project are expressed means that one must speak the language of the

> employees, not the management. At the heart of sensitive projects there is the basic fact that the project is meant to solve our problems, not those of the others.

SEVERAL LATERAL PROJECTS MIGHT BE NECESSARY FOR THE SAME PROJECT

Experience shows that sometimes it is difficult to formulate a single lateral project which suits all players. It can be easier to launch many lateral projects which, when combined, guarantee a successful outcome for the original project. So, if a large supermarket chain wants to centralise its buying function, there could be three attendant lateral projects:

- Getting those in charge of filling shelves to become more focused on product display and sales, rather than simple shelf-filling.
- Mobilise the buyers at head office to become more aware and responsive to the needs of the shops.
- Install a new computer system to link the shops, head office and the warehouses to ensure better service and supply.

So the project to centralise buying will mean something specific to each of the groups which will interest and attract them. The lateral project strategy does not try to impose the same project – even if formulated differently – on everyone. It aims to mobilise allies, each within the lateral project that concerns them, on the specific issues that matter to them. It is very rare to have one lateral project. Most likely there will be many lateral projects each responding to the specifications of allies who have, necessarily, different expectations.

To impose a project is to impose one's own project. By allowing each group of allies to formulate its own project one will give the whole a greater flexibility than by trying to obtain a consensus at any cost, which is impossible anyway on one single project. In practical terms, when everything in the world is in a state of crisis, how can one create this dynamic? Two ideas will provide a guide:

1. the need to have a third party intervene to get away from the players' existing behaviours, which are naturally flawed because they are in crisis; and
2. respect for the principles of group dynamics.

THE NEED FOR A THIRD PARTY

The strategy of the lateral project does not merely take into account the motivation of the players, it also assumes the existence of relationships between people. If the project to be launched is difficult, it is because these relationships are at best distant, and at worst atrocious.

How can competing projects be brought closer together, despite negative preconceived notions which are often ingrained in the minds of the players involved? The originators of the project are in the worst position to do this. Their presence is often enough to bring to the surface these preconceived notions, which are deep-seated and latent.

It is then that the third party intervenes. In a field of play with tense relationships, the agendas are so fixed that it is no longer possible to make the relationships evolve.

The intervention of a third party is needed to bring about a change in behaviour. Edward de Bono says that in practical terms a third person can do much to modify a hostile atmosphere, whereas the parties involved cannot do very much. This is called *mediation*. This process of calling into question actual relationships, can only function if the third party has the sole and unique role of finding a consensual outcome.

Whatever happens, such work can never be undertaken by the team which launched the original project. Edward de Bono remarks:

> The parties involved in a conflict may actually be in the worst position to resolve that conflict – except where the outcome is to be determined by force. I want to emphasize that I do not consider this due to ill will or greed on the part of those involved. It is the logic of the situation and it could not be otherwise. To expect from a combatant the heroics of complete disclosure and complete faith in the other party is to expect stupidity.

Of course de Bono was referring to conflicts, but these comments are also true of sensitive projects even when there is no conflict at the beginning. He quotes a number of reasons to call in a third party:

- The function of the third party is to *transform a two-dimensional discussion into a three-dimensional exploration, leading to a solution.* One is naturally blinded by the strengths of one's own arguments and so one does not pay enough attention to the ideas of others, even when they are right. Popular wisdom states: 'No one is deafer than

those who do not want to listen'. The third party's role is to draw attention to new ideas that had been unnoticed.
- When there is a deadlock it often comes from the approach which was used before the project was launched and which is likely to continue. *To change relationships between people,* there must be someone outside the system who proposes different scenarios, different atmospheres, other ways of reasoning or proceeding. Quite often a third party only brings to the project another way of doing things and, sometimes, this simple move is enough to solve the problem.
- The third party, technically, is not involved in the project and therefore has no interest in one solution over another. So he or she can *be provocative* and thereby find solutions without raising the level of tension.

The authors' experience on sensitive projects has led them to realise that, *the less they know about the subject at the beginning, the better their work will be.* The reverse is that if the sector is well-known to them, they will be obliged to defend a position which they believe to be the right one. In that case, it is better to hand the project to another consultant who is untainted by 'original sin'.

TO CREATE A GROUP DYNAMIC

The arrival of a third party in a field of players is not sufficient to relieve long-standing tensions. To create a group dynamic around a lateral project, the third party must respect some general principles that apply to group dynamics. The third party must also follow a 'process', that is to say, a series of linked stages whose purpose is to get the group to take charge of itself.

In a classical project, the word 'stage' often points to a series of actions whose purpose is to reach a 'milestone'. In the case of a sensitive project the milestone might only be the state of mind of the players. To construct the stages of the process to be implemented, two aspects must be differentiated: private meetings and group meetings. Players do not adopt the same attitudes when they meet face to face and when they are in a group. The face-to-face meeting allows one to penetrate more deeply into the other's *personal agenda.* The group meeting shows the socially acceptable state of the relationship. There is no more truth in one or the other state, but most deadlocks come from differences between those states. There is little point in finding allies if they are not capable at a precise moment – called 'revelation' – to band together so that they can acknowledge that they are allies.

There is a formidable power in the conjunction of both techniques: the private discussion and the group meeting. Putting in place a group dynamic generally involves *a series of stages alternating between the individual stimuli of the players and the collective stimuli of the same players.*

For example, mediation–revelation, which will be described in the next chapter, starts with a series of individual interviews. These allow one to know the positions of the players, on a one-to-one basis. The next step consists of announcing to the group what was said at these individual meetings without, of course, stating who said what. That has a quasi-magical effect on people. Suddenly they accept what they had never accepted before. This process which we will call revelation allows one to create a collective dynamism for a project.

What is important is not that allies agree, but that they act together. The agreement, the consensus, are static states of a group. The project is a dynamic state. For the group dynamism to endure, one must lead the group through a common work method which – when it is created – structures the project in time. *The strength of the allies' support comes from the process that puts them in this dynamic flow.*

For example, it is not because the board members of a company are in favour of a project that the project is going to succeed. They must also accept the process of implementing this project with regular meetings with employees so that progress can be monitored by both sides. What has to be 'sold' is not just the project but the way of doing it, that is why this process is called *animating the project,* which is explored later in the book.

POINTS TO REMEMBER

- The strategy to be adopted by the leaders of sensitive projects is similar to the herdsman strategy:
  o identifying one's potential allies;
  o mobilising and organising them so they can act together;
  o giving them the means to convince others and trusting them to find the right way;
  o there will then be time to deal with those left behind.

What is perceived as collective energy is the sum of the energy of the organised players. Therefore, the objective of the sensitive project is to help one's allies to be organised.

- Allies are more amenable to organising themselves for their own project, that is, a lateral project.
- Several lateral projects may be needed for any one original project.
- A project is often difficult because the relationships between the players are difficult. One needs a third party to intervene in order genuinely to change the players' behaviour.
- To create a group dynamic around a lateral project, a third party must respect the general principles of the dynamic of the group:
  - the group dynamic process follows stages of individual stimulation of the players with stages of collective stimulation of the same players;
  - for the group dynamism to endure, one must lead the group through a common work method, which, when it is created, structures the project in time.

8 Launching the First Circle

In order to get a sensitive project off the ground, a limited group of allies must be dynamically focused on a lateral project. This group is the first circle from which successive circles of players can be mobilised. To create and develop this first dynamic of the group the authors have developed an approach called 'mediation–revelation'.

This generally follows five steps, although real events can complicate this basic outline:

- *Step 1* Identify the waverers and the golden triangles.
- *Step 2* Meet each of them and ask them to express their feelings about the project.
- *Step 3* Abstract and synthesise the content of these meetings and build a lateral project adapted to the needs of people who have been met.
- *Step 4* From those who have been met, invite the allies to form a group in order to listen to the synthesis of the meetings carried out by the mediator. The 'revelation' effect starts off a dynamic, an action process.
- *Step 5* Stay with the team to realise their 'lateral project'.
- *Step 1* (repeated) Start again with a new circle.

Let's focus on each step and describe it more precisely.

STEP 1: IDENTIFYING POTENTIAL ALLIES WHO ARE WAVERING

This step consists of identifying for a given group (for example, truckers, mayors or supervisors) the golden triangles and/or the waverers. One will avoid having only waverers in the group; this network of allies must not be passive. One expects actions from allies and neither passives nor, even more so, opponents can act.

This survey of the players is carried out on the basis of 'segmenting the field of play' (Chapter 2). Initially, this does not have to be particularly precise. *The objective is not to mobilise all the allies at once, but to form the first circle* so that others can be added to it progressively to enlarge this first circle.

The aim is to identify a reasonable number of people, about a dozen – at least more than five (below five it is not a group) and no more than twenty (above twenty it is not a group, but a crowd). But why only meet potential allies? This partisan approach shocks a lot of theoreticians. They believe it is biased because one does not obtain an objective overview as everyone's views are not taken into account.

First, the purpose of the exercise is not to have an objective view of the situation, but to get a group to move. At this stage a comprehensive view is not particularly helpful. Second, experience shows that opponents criticise but do not propose anything. To know what is not going to work is of no interest. What is interesting is to understand what needs to be done in order for things to work. So, there is no need to have opponents in the sample. The third reason for our 'biased' sample is to take the temperature. This is in itself an action on the system. The simple act of meeting opponents runs the risk of provoking a reaction.

This principle, that measuring is never neutral, is the basis of the mediation–revelation system. In sensitive projects one cannot send someone to undertake an investigation to form a decision which is then acted upon. The simple fact that one is measuring is, in itself, provoking a change to the system. So, in order to do this, it makes obvious sense to favour allies and leave opponents alone. Finally, the rarest resource is time. One must devote those rare resources to one's allies rather than one's opponents.

STEP 2: DOING THE ROUNDS

The second step consists of individual meetings with the allies who were identified in the exercise to segment the field of play. This is what General Petain did when he took charge of the French army which he accomplished merely by 'doing the rounds': simply meeting soldiers on the battleground and listening to their complaints.

The objective of these meetings is to note for each individual:

- *The positive points* that individuals find in the project and the reasons why they believe it should go ahead. One is always surprised by the reasons why people support or would support a project. One discovers, each time, arguments that are not only new, but which are often more meaningful to the target population than those used by the project initiator.

Thus, in an information technology project several people said: 'It's perfect. With a portable computer, I will install games for my children'. This remark incensed the IT director who immediately tried to prevent the installation of games on the hard disk. Yet, this was a good argument for the computers and was successfully used later.

- *The complaints* about the project, that is the criticisms – justified or unjustified – people have about the project. To list the criticisms is interesting in itself: one discovers new ones which no one had thought of. In another information technology project it was discovered that the network had a breakdown rate significantly higher than that reported by the IT director, because he counted breakdowns in a different way from the users. This exercise also makes conversations less tense: the mediator, to play his or her role, must keep a certain distance from the project. *To listen with attention to criticisms, even the worst ones, without answering them and without seeming shocked allows the interviewee really to enter into the discussion.*
- *The conditions or demands for the project to be implemented.* This is the fundamental point of the whole process. First, it leads people to put themselves in the position of a buyer. As every salesperson knows, the key moment in the buyer's decision-making process is when he or she envisions that the product has been bought. For example, buyers will have reservations, not of the principle but of the practicalities. About the sofa, they may say: 'but my lounge is too small', instead of saying: 'I don't need a sofa'. By setting out conditions about the implementation of a project, the interviewees are beginning to accept it. One is already in the situation of achieving it.

Finally, it allows one to identify the project's 'lateralities'. As in the IT project quoted above, it was realised that the computer would not fit on the desks of the sales-force. This revealed that there were ergonomic problems with the desks, which in turn led to the uncovering of a laterality of the project: improving the working conditions of the sales force was a powerful motivational factor.

By offering the possibility to lay down conditions, the project is no longer something fixed to be accepted or refused: *it is something to build* and the interviewee is ready to do it. The key sentence to listen for during the interview is: 'Hey, do you think that this will be possible?' Meaning: 'It is a revelation for me that this condition could be acceptable, even possible', which shows that interest has been raised.

There is an absolutely fundamental point here: 'Doing the rounds' of meetings is not a mere data collection exercise. It is not just a temperature-gauging operation. It is a communication activity whose objective is to *create an expectation within the people who have been met.* In fact, it becomes impossible to stop the process once it has started. Indeed, the result would be even more catastrophic if the process were stopped because an expectation would have been created in the players, an expectation which would not have been satisfied.

STEP 3: BUILDING A LATERAL PROJECT

As a result of 'doing the rounds' one has two types of data:

- A verification of the field of play and each player's sociodynamic position; and
- A list showing each player's stance or position towards the project and their lateralities.

Verifying the sociodynamic position of the players is important. Effectively players are chosen on the impressions one had of them at the start, but the meetings allow one to get to know their real agenda, and in particular the degree of synergy: Is an individual making proposals? Are there conditions? Are there demands?

For example, the annual evaluation interviews in a civil service department are a particularly sensitive subject. The central director of administration had been nominated for the pilot study group because he was, theoretically, extremely open to human resources problems. In particular he was a specialist in transactional analysis (something quite uncommon at that level of the civil service). However, at the end of the thorough interview with the authors it was obvious he was highly inflexible and locked into some ineffective concepts (sociodynamics measure -4) and incapable of making any proposals (sociodynamics measure $+1$). He was an opponent dressed as an ally ($+1, -4$).

One can also, during these rounds of meetings, discover a key player one had not considered. For example, the president of the Sports Club in a large company had considerable influence and turned out to be an ally of a sensitive project.

But, of course, what is particularly important is *the quality of the list of the players' positions and their lateralities,* since it is this list which will enable one to build a lateral project – which adds to the original project – which will stir people into action. In order to analyse positions the win/win diagram (see Figure 8.1) is used, which prepares the ground for the lateral project. This diagram classifies the proposals along two axes:

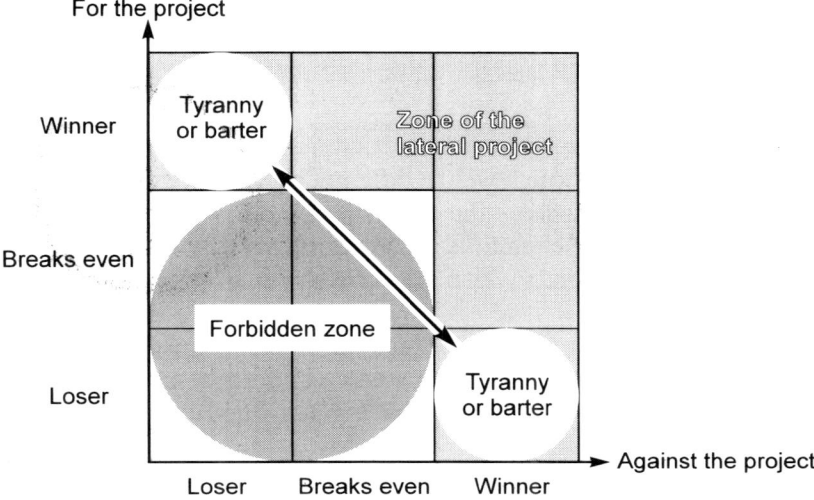

Figure 8.1 The win/win diagram

- on the y-axis are the interests of the initiator of the project: we are winners/we break even/we are losers;
- on the x-axis are the interests of the population concerned: the player is a winner/the player breaks even/the player is a loser.

This diagram enables one to identify three types of proposals:

- *The forbidden proposals* – those where one party loses without having the other win anything.
- *The dilemma* – proposals where one party loses but the other clearly wins. These proposals are called dilemmas because there is doubt about the interests of the people involved: either one compensates in some way the one who accepts a loss, in which case one could be in a win/win exchange; or, and this is more common, the loser will find his or her own compensation which will destroy the advantage gained by the other. An example illustrates this mechanism: a company wanted to reduce the commissions of its sales force due to difficult trading conditions. That put the company in a winning position, but the sales force loses out. Six months later not only had the sales force lost in terms of salary but the turnover had also decreased – a lose/lose relationship. Without fully understanding why, it often appears that a lose/win situation soon becomes after a while, a lose/lose situation!

- *Win/win proposals* – these are the proposals which allow one to formulate a lateral project, where both parties win something, or at least lose nothing.

With the list of players' positions and lateralities, the task is to reconstruct a lateral project which will be different from the original. However, this new project must include the old project, more or less 'revisited', and it takes into account the remarks made during the interviews. It can also include totally new aspects which are necessary to develop the synergy of the allies.

The Euralille project, that is the renewal of Lille's town centre around the new TGV train station, could be seen as a laterality of the Eurotunnel project. These two projects are distinct, but without Euralille those in favour of the Eurotunnel project would most probably not have had such a strong ally as the Nord-Pas-de-Calais region. Without Euralille, Eurotunnel might not have happened.

The formulation of a lateral project is not simple. In Part III, there is an analysis of the precautions to be taken and the method to be followed.

STEP 4: ORGANISING THE LAUNCH MEETING (REVELATION AND COMMITMENT)

As previously seen there can be many allies, but the battle can still be lost if they stay dispersed and isolated. The processes to mobilise allies must go through a collective moment. It is this collective, this mass meeting or assembly, that selects the choice of the majority and carries their values.

If a consensus appears, one must organise for it to be expressed in a collective process in order for it to be ratified. This is the object of the revelation/commitment meeting. This meeting can take numerous forms. It could be a one-day seminar for those in the first circle so they can form a pilot group charged with steering the project. Or it could be an extremely formal meeting with important elected representatives and strict protocol. One must adapt to circumstances. The principle consists of gathering the players met by the third party and of having them follow a process of collective development which leads to a commitment by each person on what to do next with the lateral project.

This meeting is not a jolly. At this stage of the process the players have not met each other in the context of the lateral project. When they arrive at the meeting, they are still locked in to the position they took after the launch of the original project. In order to achieve the objective of the meeting – to generate a positive collective dynamic for the project – the meeting must follow a structured process consisting of four successive well-identified time periods.

Period 1: Clearing the Minefield

In this type of meeting it is important to emphasise that which is constructive and to limit the effect of that which is destructive. Paradoxically, in order to do this it is unnecessary to hide what upsets people. On the contrary, the meeting must start by reminding everyone of the existing sources of tension (if there are any). It is as though a purification must take place before the collective reconstruction process can occur. This is *clearing the minefield.*

The authors are always fascinated by how incredibly efficient this is. The simple fact that a third party can raise, in front of the group, the criticisms which have been levelled at one person, one project, one group *without that person interrupting,* has an almost miraculous effect on relationships. On the other hand, every time that one is persuaded not to raise the problems that exist in the relationship – often because it is insulting or very personal – the mine explodes soon after, destroying what had been built.

Clearing the minefield might only involve some small points in the eyes of the project leader, but it is precisely because these points seem minor to those in charge that they are sources of tension. For example, if one of the players is sensitive to the management style of a manager because he or she is impolite or does not do what he or she promises, it must be said, or at least the words must be found to say it. If there is any doubt about any aspect of the project it must be aired, even if it is a well-guarded secret.

This method of working is made easier by the third party who can describe the tensions just as so many communication problems. It allows for the relationship to be rationalised, so making it more transparent and more acceptable for all the people involved. The clearing of mines must be full but brief. It will not be necessary for everyone to restate the problems, as is usually the case with this type of meeting: this is already done by the external experts.

The clearing of mines also allows the reconstruction stage to be reached quickly and the meeting can come straight to proposals. The advantage of having chosen allies to participate in the meeting becomes clear: the quick move to concrete proposals is easier. The presence of opponents in the room would have made this step much more difficult.

Period 2: Revealing the Lateral Project

The second key moment of the meeting is the revelation of the lateral project. The term 'revelation' might seem a bit evangelical. However, it reflects the effect that must be obtained to break the cycle of knee-jerk reactions which are the result of deeply ingrained interpersonal relationships.

Often one is tempted to test the concepts which are to be presented before the meeting to gauge their acceptability. This is a mistake. It removes the element of surprise which is important because it destabilises, and this destabilisation is the result which is wanted. Already, the clearing of mines has itself been a surprise and has caused destabilisation, but this destabilisation is not enough because it doesn't offer a constructive way out. The revelation brings, on the contrary, a *constructive destabilisation*, what will be called later in the book a credible *way out*.

Period 3: Discussion/Tuning

People do not immediately understand the lateral project, especially if it disturbs their beliefs. First they hear what is new. Before they can commit themselves they must first absorb the consequences of the change. Only then will they really start to understand.

If this level of understanding is not checked, the result can be substantive disagreements. Just because the participants in the meeting say they have understood does not mean that they really have. The best means to accelerate this conscious realisation is to make them work on the proposed concepts and ideas. After the lateral project is revealed, it is not sufficient to say: 'Well, what do you think?' The group must be led to take over the project. For example, this can be done by working with them on a solid theme: 'How do we present this to the employees?' Then the real outline of the project begins to form in people's minds.

Period 4: The Collective Commitment on a Work Process

The objective of this whole process is not just to obtain agreement from the participants, but also to get a collective commitment. This commitment has two functions: first, to lock in everyone's mind, through solid facts, a real acceptance of the dynamic of the project. Second to ensure that this commitment is made in front of everyone. The disapproving glance of a colleague is not only a powerful motivational factor, it is also a punishment factor.

Collective commitment must relate not just to the project but to a work process. If the meeting was well led there will be, in effect, a formal individual commitment from the participants. This descriptive unfolding of the revelation might seem rather theoretical; in reality it is always more complex.

However, experience shows how indispensable these four time periods are. The absence of one reduces the efficiency of the rest and the order must be respected otherwise disaster strikes. On the other hand, it is possible that these stages might be spread over a longer period of time.

STEP 5: MAINTAINING THE DYNAMIC

As a result of Step 4 a network of allies has been formed. A group of players has decided to work together towards the same objective. This objective could be small, such as an agreement to meet regularly to discuss the project, or large, for example to take charge of a part of the project. So, depending on the project, there will be a steering committee, a project committee, a follow-up committee, a watchdog committee, a discussion group or some other structure representing an 'institutionalisation' of the process.

According to this plan, the term committee not only describes the meeting of the people concerned ('the management committee meets every Monday at 6.00 p.m.'). It also establishes a management system that is both a network of players – acting in accordance with the project to which they have agreed (individual action) – and also a source from which they receive regular support and the opportunity to discuss actions (collective action).

Once the network of relationships with allies is established in a given area, it is vital to bring the process to life. This is all that the promoters of the project need to do, since the objective of this network is to carry out the actions that it cannot or does not want to undertake. Part IV of this book will be dedicated to the way of maintaining this dynamic without replacing the players.

Step 1 (again): Do it Again with a New Group

The mediation–revelation method does not just function on a homogenous area. Its objective is, of course, to create a network of allies, but in a progressive manner; covering the field of players and getting the project back on track cannot all be done at once. On the contrary, it is by multiplying the networks created and by connecting them that one can cover, step by step, the field of the play of the project. One must first develop networks to the side and below.

On the Side

Here several fields of play are tackled which do not have direct links: they are independent of each other. The information spreads with the involvement of the project team. For example, if the truck drivers are convinced, elected representatives are tackled next, when they are convinced, the doctors are next and then the academics, and so on. If the sales force is convinced, the administration section is next and when they are convinced, the marketing department will be next, etc.

Underneath

Here only one field is tackled and by convincing a first circle of allies at the top of the pyramid, they are encouraged to convince other circles of allies underneath. Thus the information spreads from the top to the bottom of the field. For example, once the local councillors are mobilised, the next to be convinced are the local mayors, and then the members of parliament, etc. Another example of the mobilisation process: first the management committee, then the department heads, then the client account managers, then the secretaries, etc.

At the beginning of this chapter it was clear that every move had the potential to cause an 'explosion', the best allies had started to turn their backs on the project and it was impossible to see how it could progress. By using the mediation–revelation process, based on the strategy of allies, this has led to:

- *a better understanding of the causes of the difficulties* encountered and some pointers on how to avoid recurrences;
- *a better understanding of the forces at work* – the mediation–revelation process has uncovered factors which allow a better division of the field of play to provide a better map of allies and opponents;
- *more importantly, a first circle of allies has been involved* and they have decided to work together; and
- *there is a common project, a lateral project*, which is believed to be a more attractive project for the rest of the population. The project manifests itself in some very concrete actions – a work plan – that will have to be followed in future.

Launching the First Circle

Once the network of allies has stabilised, it should be possible to resume the project. However, it soon becomes apparent that only the easiest part of the task has been completed: the overall objective is to enlarge the circle of allies and progressively to occupy the whole of the area.

POINTS TO REMEMBER

- The mediation–revelation process is a system of five steps whose objective is to create the first dynamic towards achieving the initial project through the lateral project.
- The first circle of allies must contain at least five, and at most twenty players, consisting of golden triangles and waverers.
- The round of meetings must identify 'lateralities' that have the potential to win over the first circle and others.
- The synthesis meeting must follow a precise agenda beginning with the clearing of mines and leading to an individual commitment on a work method.
- The dynamic created by the mediation–revelation process must be renewed to cover, possibly through numerous lateral projects, the whole field of the players.

Part III
Conceiving a Lateral Project

So far consideration of the lateral project has been rather sketchy. A quick skim could mislead the reader into thinking that this phase is quite mechanical, and that it consists of choosing between different perspectives of a project depending on its degree of acceptability to allies. One could conclude that this is simply a matter of cosmetics.

The role of the lateral project is not to reformulate the project but to reconceive it, depending on the energy one perceives in the players. This part of the book gives a number of pointers on how to do this. The following chapter shows that the lateral project is more a state of mind to be maintained throughout the project rather than a particular phase of the project. One simply cannot conceive the lateral project as a unique event and then manage it as if the project were of Type 1.

EXPLAINING ONESELF DOES NOT ALWAYS SOLVE THE PROBLEMS

The authors learnt their trade in a firm of management consultants. In this demanding and rigorous culture, the focus is placed on respecting facts and their detailed description. Facts are facts. In order to make ourselves understood and to succeed in implementing change, one must distinguish every fact using words that are both precise and technically justified. Truth is unique and always good to tell.

Armed with such principles, one of the authors' first experiences was at the request of the staff representative committee (works council) of a large company.

An Abortive Attempt at Explaining: The Case of a Company's Staff Representative Committee

In many European countries, the staff representative committee (elected democratically by the employees) can, under certain conditions, ask for an expert to be nominated to evaluate the effects of a management proposal. We were retained by the SRC of a large service group and we went about our investigations in the normal way, even when tension in the air made data collection a little arduous.

We wrote our report and presented it to our clients – the elected representatives of the committee. This went very badly. The presentation was stopped at every word. Our clients uncovered hidden meanings in the report which we had never intended. Contritely, we returned with a rewritten report taking into account the highly pertinent remarks made by the committee. Frankly, we didn't change anything fundamental, but we did develop the format. Eventually a formulation evolved that was as satisfying to ourselves as to the employees' representatives.

We then presented the modified report to the management committee, made up of five directors, all graduates of top universities. The presentation started at 9 o'clock, and at noon we were still there. Once again, we were stopped at every word. The formulation which we had worked on word by word and which we believed to be fair was causing problems. Listening to the directors, whilst trying to distinguish well-thought-out remarks from insults, we discovered that our report could have yet another meaning than the one intended.

This game lasted two months. We finally presented an oral report to the staff representative committee. It didn't mean much but it satisfied everyone.

Evaluation

This contract cost a lot of time and anguish, but it reveals some aspects of the management of sensitive projects. One aspect has already been discussed at length: when 'the bosses' are on one side and the 'workers' on the other, the task is more complicated as two camps materialise with each trying to impose its point of view on the other. This is not a clever working method. We have seen that the mediation–revelation process strives not to identify two camps in order to avoid fixed positions.

This example also demonstrates two key aspects of the strategy of the lateral project:

1. The formulation of facts and situations is a difficult task, because words and phrasing have a different meaning according to the people to which they are addressed. *To speak does not necessarily solve problems, but it can worsen them.* Goodwill is not sufficient.
2. To merely reformulate the project – as we tried to do – leads to a dead end. *To convince people, they must justifiably believe they can modify the project and adapt it to their reality.* Whoever supports the project must accept this. In the case of the staff representative committee the two camps were entrenched in their positions. The management wanted to implement an ambitious technical project that would greatly enhance the role of the engineers. For them the change was natural and communication to others was almost an after-thought. The unions wanted to preserve jobs and make the over-confident engineers, who had little respect for the workers, knuckle under.

There was no consensus on the formulation simply because there was no consensual project. This part of the book does not deal with the *formulations* of a lateral project, even if one dissects the words and phrases, it deals with the *conception*. This 'reconception' of the original project must follow five principles:

- taking the irrational into account;
- do not respect time, respect timing;
- going for broke;
- have allies write the lateral project; and
- move from penalties to benefits.

9 Taking the Irrational into Account

RESISTANCE AND MISUNDERSTANDING

To allow for the irrational is one of the most revealing aspects of the strategy of the lateral project. There has already been mention of some aspects of the management of sensitive projects which do not belong to logic. This was the case when the changes in behaviour of players under stress was examined or when group dynamic techniques in the mediation–revelation process were discussed. But experience shows that the most difficult concept for players to accept is the attempt to introduce them to a rationality different from their own. It is, however, one of the key points in the construction of the lateral project that mobilises energies effectively. To illustrate this difficulty, let's start with an example.

Some Amazing Resistance to Change: The Insurance Case

An insurance company decides to computerise its accident claims department. This department handles accident files, compiled from the declaration forms of the policy holder, until the case is closed. Tasks include: checking documents, evaluating damages, managing external interventions, follow-up of legal procedures, paying experts, lawyers and bailiffs, and so on.

It is organised in groups each consisting of 15 writers. Each group is managed by a level-V writer (the highest in grade with a law degree and experience), surrounded by some level-IV writers (who also have a law degree but are less experienced), and a dozen level-III writers (with a good general education and about two years' experience) (see Figure 9.1).

Every morning the files arrive on the desks of the level-V writers. They distribute the work to the troops depending on their skills. Simple files go to level-III writers, complex files to level-IV writers. The big accidents are kept with the level-V writers. Each writer assumes responsibility for all aspects of the file until it is closed.

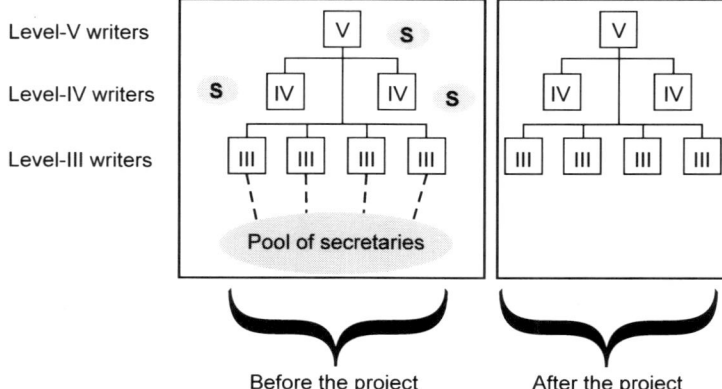

Figure 9.1 Organisational structure of the accident claims department

Before computerisation, the work of the 'accident' groups had two strong characteristics:

- First, writers work in pairs, each with a secretary who deals with administration (file handling, sorting, planning of calls, and so on). The writer is in charge of relationships with the outside world and is the legal expert. The writers organise themselves with 'their' secretaries.
- Second, writing is king. No wonder the position is called writer: writing is the essential quality for the job: phrasing a letter, doing a calculation, drafting a report.

The computerisation of the group is scheduled to happen in two phases:

- phase 1: the removal of level-III writers' secretaries;
- phase 2: the removal of level-IV writers' secretaries.

The first phase goes without a hitch. Computer terminals are installed on the writers' desks. These computers are linked to a central database that holds the complete file history and it is accessible to everyone. The arrival of electronic mail and other computer programmes means many procedures and correspondence become standardised. Many of the administrative tasks of sorting and transmitting information are automated and paper is avoided whenever possible.

Before computerisation secretaries spent much of their time coming and going to the archives, which led to many 'breaks for a chat'. With computerisation, everything is available on the screen in real time: level-III writers can work on their own.

The change is smooth for level-III writers. At this level, in practice, no secretary was specifically dedicated to a writer since they worked in a pool. Level-III writers see computerisation as an improvement of their status and of their skills. It also gives them more freedom in the management of files (they do not have to rely on a pool of secretaries who are often poorly motivated, all the more so as many of the secretaries believe they could do the level-III writers' jobs themselves).

The project now moves to the next phase: computerisation of the level-IV writers' secretaries. This second phase of the project goes badly. Without exception the level-IV writers refuse to accept the change. To the surprise of the top management, this second phase of the project leads to two bitter conflicts with strong periods of tension in between. This affects all the writers and leaves the management in a state of shock for two years. These conflicts are made worse as they involve senior staff who are the future management of the company.

Evaluation

Why is it that which was welcomed by the level-III writers created so much tension for level-IV writers?

It became rapidly apparent that this conflict was the result of a series of misunderstandings and of more or less well-founded intentions. The different parties did not communicate at any one time on the same wavelength.

- The top management speaks of *efficiency*, of adapting to the computer programmes, of technical solutions, of cost-objectives geared towards competitors.
- The writers speak of *human relations*, of status, of the skills of being a writer, of respect for the human being, of respect for the law, of the nice surroundings, of warmth, of trust, of 'hand-crafted' expertise.

The problem is how to get the top management to comprehend that the real cause of the conflict is that they do not understand what makes the writers tick. There is, however, an easy way out, a 'lateral project' that could be easily implemented if the top management could agree to the need to enter into a human, emotive process and not a technical one.

Every time this is raised with the top management they respond with shock: how can the employees not see that the future of the company is more important than their 'petty little existential problems!'

This type of communication problem often appears obvious to a third party who comes in without any preconceptions. The challenge is not to understand, *but to get this analysis accepted by people when it deeply offends their view of the world.* One looks for a way of describing people's motivations so that they work for the project rather than against it.

RATIONALISING THE IRRATIONAL USING THE VUD GRID

The grid that is used to achieve this comes from transactional analysis. It is simple to understand and thus to share. It is called the VUD grid (see Figure 9.2), for Value, Usefulness, Desire, and is analogous to the PAC (Parent, Adult, Child) model developed by Eric Berne, who developed transactional analysis.

As seen earlier, players are characterised by the energy they can devote to a project. Transactional analysis focuses on the origins of this energy,

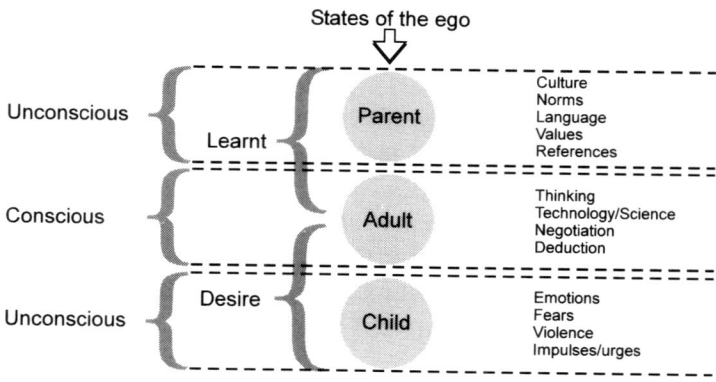

Figure 9.2 States of the ego in transactional analysis

and it is based on the principle that the behaviour of individuals results from two factors:

1. *Desires*, or what transactional analysis regards as a person's Child, because it is the dominant part of the personality of the child. Desire is energy. It creates movement: I want to play, I will get up and I am going dancing.
2. *Values,* that is the rules that he or she has learned to respect. Transactional analysis calls this part of the personality the Parent, because parents are generally at the origin of most rules.

Values do not create energy, they restrain it. Thus, we have learned that we can go dancing but only on Fridays and Saturdays, because we can sleep late the next morning: this is a value.

Desires and values are mostly unconscious, that is, not expressible in a voluntary manner with words. Berne characterises a third type of opinion in an individual, which he calls the Adult. This is the vision of the usefulness people have of things and people. The Adult is a part of one's opinions, that is, of one's desires and values. The Adult represents the part that one can talk about and express in front of others, that is finally accepted. This difference between what one thinks and what one authorises oneself to think generates the *behaviours of substitution.* For example, we will not allow ourselves suddenly to feel like going to a disco during office hours.

However, that won't prevent us from having such a hidden desire deep inside, in our Child, that will influence our behaviour. We might then possibly have a headache and ask for a coffee break which will seem like an acceptable demand. We can rationalise this and we can convince ourselves – and others – that the break was helpful. We will then be in the Adult mode whilst the origin of the demand will be in our Child.

It is possible, therefore, to represent each player's opinion about a project according to these three different and complementary levels of perception: values, usefulness and desires – this is the VUD model.

Values

The values of individuals are all those unconscious norms and rules which are obeyed unconsciously. The language, that is the meaning of the words – in the denotative and the connotative senses – belongs to his or her Parent. (The denotative sense of a word brings together the fundamental and permanent elements of the meaning. The connotative sense is the bringing together of variable subjective values which that word has for an individual. Everyone knows that a cemetery is a place where the dead are buried, the denotative meaning. But for John the cemetery is where he flirted with Julie, every time he thinks of the cemetery he thinks of Julie. This is the connotative sense of the cemetery for John.)

The Values of the Level-IV Writers

Level-IV writers do not type, they 'get their secretaries to do it'. So a project that assumes that level-IV writers type is going to hurt the norms deeply established within them, within their secretaries and even in those surrounding the writer.

This norm will not be expressed by saying, 'I'm losing prestige'. They will say, 'This is not efficient'. To respond to this concern with arguments, no matter how well founded (usefulness), won't be enough to change their behaviour. Values resist the logic of reason.

Evaluation

The conflict generated by the top management's wish to get level-IV writers to type clearly shows the vicious circle the players can get themselves into: level-IV writers do not speak of their true problems, because these are unconscious. Worse, if they were conscious they would be unacceptable, even for them. So, they compensate by speaking of 'the lack of efficiency of the system' (the response time is too slow, the system is inefficient for writing letters and does not adapt to real situations, there are compatibility problems between computer files and paper files, and so on). The top management is going to respond technically because it only wants to hear technical problems. Being very efficient with its mistakes, management is going to tackle each problem one by one. Of course every time a problem is solved, a new one will appear. This is the road which leads to a lose/lose project.

Usefulness

Usefulness for an individual is his or her conscious opinions. Usefulness is, in principle rational and therefore negotiable. For example, more work can be exchanged in return for a higher salary, or more skilled working can be traded for more training. People will move to a nondescript suburban industrial estate from a trendy city centre location, if the office is bigger and the train-line more convenient.

Of course, the expressed usefulness is in fact desires and norms, but these desires and norms can be expressed and so negotiated. Everyone negotiates with some of their desires ('I am on a diet') or with certain of our norms ('I will dress as a clown for a fancy dress party, but I am not a clown'). These negotiable desires and norms are considered as *usefulness*.

Desires

The desires of individuals are the most hidden. Desire is the engine while the norm is the steering wheel. Desire is our energy. It is also the most difficult part of the personality to understand. One can understand quite quickly the system of norms of individuals because it comes from their backgrounds. They can be approached by understanding their personal background. But the vital energy is the key element of the personality. Why does one desire one thing rather than another? Why is it that in the same job with the same salary and conditions, one person works efficiently and happily while another vegetates discontentedly?

Fear is a negative desire, a repulsion. A driver of behaviour can equally be a desire of reward as much as a fear of punishment. Equipped with this knowledge we can analyse how a project which involves change can either be in harmony or in conflict with a given individual's desires, usefulness and values (see Figure 9.3). That is what we will call the VUD diagnosis of a player.

Two points are worth noting:

1. The same project is not viewed in a homogenous way and so does not generate just a single opinion, whether positive or negative. It is viewed in a complex way, even in contradictory ways, within each of the three levels of perception.
2. To say that an opinion is positive regarding a project means that it is going to generate synergy on the part of the player. The reverse holds for negative opinions.

So how would this model function, positively or negatively, in the case of the insurance company level-IV writers?

106   *Conceiving a Lateral Project*

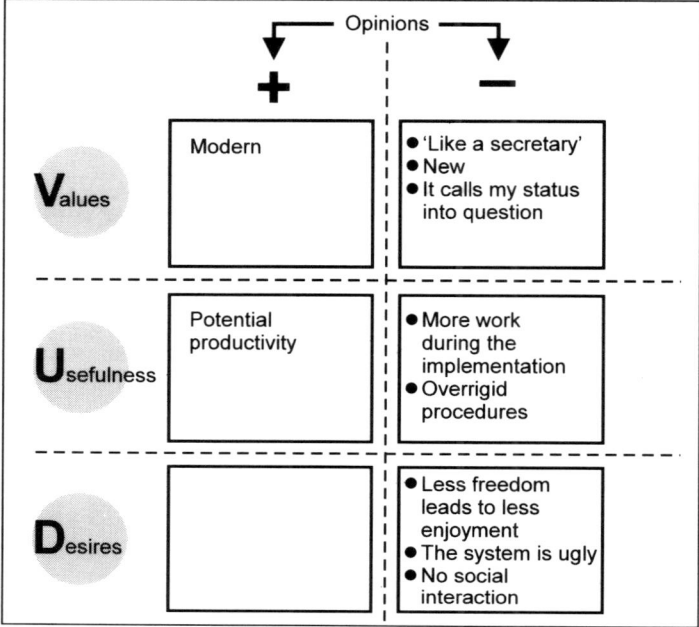

Figure 9.3 Example of the opinions of a level-IV writer to the project

The VUD Map of the Level-IV Writers' Opinions on the Computerisation of Accidents Project

This analysis should be treated with some caution as it is a caricature. Every writer has in fact a different VUD map originating from his or her personal history and character. Following a round of meetings with a sample of level-IV writers the following opinions were elicited:

1. Consistency of the Project with Level-IV Writers' Values

It has been noted that in the value system of level-IV writers the only positive aspect of this project is the fact that it is modern. Level-IV writers in this type of insurance company are generally very positive lawyers. A very strong aspect of their personality is their reference to the morality of things, that is, the struggle between good (progress) and evil (obscurantism or lack of enlightenment). The project succeeded at the beginning in connecting with the good, and this was fortunate.

However, the negative aspects are quite numerous:

- First, it is a project against writing. 'Automatic' writing is the antithesis of writing. For them the only constructive thought, therefore intelligent, is the written thought. To have standard texts is to kill the subtlety of intelligence.
- It is a project which forces them to act like their secretaries, that is to type. Now, the secretary hasn't got their knowledge, so it is a one-way ticket towards obscurantism.
- It is a new project. As noted, for the writers modernity is positive but – paradoxically – novelty is negative because it modifies the established order: the law. Opinions can be contradictory and this is the case here.
- It is a project which questions their status. The questioning of status is taken into account by the management in its legal and technical dimension, but not in its irrational dimension.

In top management culture, the word status refers to the writers' job descriptions, salaries and perks. Status is what is written in an agreement. So the management proposes some legal changes to the writers to guarantee them a higher status, the granting of a new IT qualification, and a bonus linked to the change. But it does not take into account the irrational aspect of their status, the respect of their peers, colleagues and friends. The same word means two things.

The project puts the level-IV writers, who are the élite of the company, on the same status as someone from administration. Worse, it puts them at the mercy of computer scientists who are perceived as automatons: they do not think. A level-IV writer easily quotes Kant or Shakespeare. A computer specialist reads Superman comics. (The authors would like to stress that this was the view of the level-IV writers. It was not verified!)

2. *The Usefulness of the Project for Level-IV Writers*

On the positive side:

- there are potential efficiency gains, so if clients telephone they can be updated on their situation immediately; and
- information is more readily available.

On the negative side:

- it is an added workload for the level-IV writers who will now have to type their own texts;
- procedures are too strict and so less efficient;
- the database is full of mistakes;
- there is a risk in making decisions without looking at the paper file which is the only legal proof and complete document; and
- the network often breaks down and the computer system is not reliable.

3. The Desires this Project Generates

No positive desires were found on this project. On the contrary, the negative desires are numerous:

- It is a project which *hinders the relationship with the secretary and with people in general,* and this diminishes desire for the project. Humans are by nature gregarious creatures and this project reduces the opportunity to have social contact.
- It is an ugly project and so it does not enter the field of desires: the machines are ugly, it introduces disorder into an established order, the manuals are ugly, the screens are ugly and the head of the project is ugly. A beautiful object is an object which clearly refers to pleasurable connotations, that is to *the authorisation we have to enjoy our desires.*
- It is a project which, in a fairly strict way, sets formal rules on how work should be tackled. This is *emasculating* and a very real kill-joy. The feeling of freedom is, in fact, the feeling of being able to play, that is to be allowed to express desires. Before, writers had a feeling of freedom: they could organise their work as they pleased. With this project they must follow precise procedures that are imposed by the computer. By defining the procedures very strictly and by not compensating with any other expression of freedom, a feeling of emasculation has been created.
- It is a project which *increases productivity,* and so the quality of work must fall – because it is impossible to think quickly and, at the same time, well. Work should be done in serenity, and by speeding up the rhythm there are bound to be mistakes. So there is a fear of punishment (the real sanction for level-IV writers is

> not a reprimand from the management, it is the disapproving glance of their colleagues).
> - It is a project that *dematerialises files*. This is like asking a child to play with the image of a doll rather than with an actual doll. There is no sound, no touching, no smell, no feeling of familiarity with the object. Ghosts are frightening, so is the virtual world of computing. Without files, the writers lose their bearings and so become scared.
>
> **Evaluation**
>
> Universally, there is no lack of arguments in favour of the project. What is missing are the incentives to develop the desires of the writers and a reference to their values to help them accept the project.

This example highlights three important points concerning a player's VUD diagnosis:

1. *This diagnosis is unacceptable to the writers.* It may even be unacceptable to many readers, as it is unacceptable to many clients. When the authors undertake this type of diagnosis it is not made public for two reasons:

    - It doesn't help the people listening to it, except to trouble them; and
    - It risks provoking violent rejections of the type, 'Where are you getting all this from?' or worse, 'I thought you were serious people'.

2. *It is approximate.* The authors are practitioners not psychotherapists. The purpose is to construct solutions in order to get to the objective – to develop a person's synergy. The object of the analysis is not to describe precisely the subconscious of that person, but to find solutions that will be validated by experience.

    So, for example, the fear concerning the dematerialisation of the files may have been a mis-analysis. One will find out quickly: the solution that is found to counter that fear will not work, then another lead must be sought.

3. In an analysis of the situation, the consultants are no more 'in the right' than the client or anyone else. It is not that the consultant's solutions are right and those of the clients are wrong. *It is the sum of both that is richer than each one considered separately.*

The objective is not the analysis, but the solution. How, from what has been read, can a lateral project be evolved by enriching it with connotations that will help to develop the synergy of the players?

ADAPTING A PROJECT ON THREE LEVELS

Understanding the opinions of people is a complicated matter; there is no mathematical model which provides an infallible analysis of opinions.

To rewrite the project and transform it into a lateral project, three levels of perception must be considered:

- to re-enter the framework of values accepted by the other party,
- to prove its usefulness to the other party, and
- to awaken the desires of the other party.

Proceeding by Trial and Error

Whatever is done, it will only be by trial and error. What is important is the process. It is folly to define a very elaborate strategy at the beginning, and there must be the capacity to understand that something, an impression, is being transmitted. That is not so simple.

For example, a person working in the education system must be conscious of the fact that wearing a tie can place him in the category (value) of 'being external to the educational system, and thus incapable of truly understanding the problems'. One must understand the reaction provoked by the signals one transmits: no one will come forward to say that wearing a tie is a sign. How else can one know then if not by trying?

Change Quickly Depending on the Effect Produced

One must continuously adapt what is being transmitted in light of the results observed. That is why mass media tools are not suitable: mailing

4000 copies of a leaflet is not particularly adaptable to a situation. In fact it makes relationships more rigid when, on the contrary, the emphasis should be on giving some degree of freedom. On the other hand, to have a mobile exhibition whose display panels can be changed quickly if some phrasing is deemed inappropriate, could be more efficient. Therefore the situation will always be one of trial and error. The organisation must be such that, at any moment, one can pull back from an initiative and be prepared to try something else immediately. Part IV of this book will detail some suitable methods.

Having taken these precautions, experience shows what can be done to make people desire something, to make them find something useful, or to find something that fits their values.

GENERATING DESIRE

To make a project attractive, there are four tools which work well:

1. *Create a team spirit in a game* which is a regulated competition and so is accepted as a competition (as opposed to a war or a conflict). For example, two teams can be asked to compete on the same subject. As another example, asking for volunteers for an experiment produced a far better result than choosing candidates on the basis of, say, technical merit. This means the project must be attractive and that the leading role must be given to whoever is declaring either himself or herself as a candidate rather than to the project management.
2. *In the presentation of the project, add symbols of authorised pleasure.* When the project is being presented, symbols associated with pleasure are used. What is a symbol of authorised pleasure? Examples include: having an attractive man or woman as the head of the project; creating a comfortable and warm office area with a coffee machine; using colourful brochures and avoiding technical photos.

    It is important to restrict the symbols of pleasure to those considered an acceptable codified expression of that pleasure. Everything must be done so that people can say, as has been heard on one project: 'I do not know whether you are right, but you are so friendly in this team that I will follow what you say'.
3. *Develop a social scene around the project,* so that people need to get together. Organise a meeting rather than give information over the

112   *Conceiving a Lateral Project*

   telephone; offer drinks at the end. This gives the feeling that there is life in the project.
4. *'Be there when you must be'*, that is give secondary benefits, indirect interpersonal advantages to the players who are supportive, for example: sympathy, signs of attentiveness or empathy or take into account the difficulties encountered.

These examples may be surprising in their triviality compared to the seriousness of the project. In many projects where the authors have been involved everything is very serious, very professional, very well prepared, but also particularly boring. Meantime, the opponents' meetings are good fun with a lot of life, maybe a bit unruly but 'very friendly'. And so the opponents succeed quite well in mobilising players.

The managing director of a company producing lingerie does not think twice about having advertisements showing models in brassières. Yet he will be shocked to learn that in order to introduce the new accountancy system he must also get into the same process of producing desires.

This logic is particularly difficult to accept for any project which is very technical. For example in the case of large infrastructural projects the developers will say: 'A motorway is a motorway, it is naturally attractive'. The opening of Eurotunnel to trucks illustrates quite well this type of problem.

A New Efficient but not very Attractive Product: le Shuttle

Eurotunnel is a new infrastructure, not new in the sense that it provides a means of transport between the Continent and Great Britain, but because it offers a service which was unknown until then: the carriage of trucks on trains. This service was launched with a very rational promotion of the advantages for the haulage companies and truck drivers: speed (35 minutes instead of 2 hours), cost effectiveness (precise calculations showed all the advantages that it would bring to the transport companies), regularity (no storms in the tunnel).

The opening of the service was not a success, even though things have improved since. A few months after the opening truck drivers were interviewed by a newspaper. They spoke freely about their feelings. This is what they liked about the ferry:

- 'The sea' (they have a very tiring job, and to spend an hour looking at the sea is a rare privilege);
- 'The lounge where alcohol and chips are served';
- 'The other passengers' and particularly the lady passengers they could mix with, even talk to, providing a stark contrast to their air-conditioned truck cabin or soulless service stations.

Here is what they found stressful in le Shuttle:

- The bar where they were 'stuck' is 'small and confined' (it is practically a full size wagon);
- The truck drivers are all 'herded' together;
- Nothing could be seen through the window, 'not even walls, because it is all dark and cold.'
- The trip is too short to relax.

Evaluation

It is quite clear that the 'offer' presented by le Shuttle is not suited to the sensitive nature of the truck drivers. Fortunately for Eurotunnel, and unfortunately for the truck drivers, it is not they who decide the mode of transport but their employers. There would have been advantages to Eurotunnel introducing the new service with:

- hostesses in the lounge as well as barmen (socialisation);
- live entertainment in the coach (socialisation);
- the creation of a fun atmosphere with games, etc. (game);
- the possibility of mixing people, for example by accepting hitch hikers (socialisation).

To increase the desire of a player for a project, it is of paramount importance to foster pleasure and mental satisfaction.

So, for example, if one is presenting a major new roads project to a local politician, it is important that the road is placed in the context of 'major national infrastructural development' which his community can be proud of having a part in. Large glossy maps, with big arrows showing the strategic importance of the proposal, add to the sense of satisfaction and pleasure.

GIVING THE PROJECT USEFULNESS

Usefulness is developed by structured arguments. What is most difficult in this exercise is to construct arguments as a response to the players' preoccupations and not as a response to one's own logic. Generally the project initiators behave as if their logic must be imposed on everyone. Yet, arguments which are valid for some players will make others recoil.

There are even reasons for supporting a project that might not seem reasonable at first sight, but they are more meaningful for the players than all the technically sound explanations. For example, there is little point in using cost-effectiveness as an argument in favour of the project if one is speaking to someone who is worried about redundancies.

RESPECTING VALUES

René Girard showed why and how norms generate themselves through imitation. Others are imitated to the extent that they are considered as a Parent. In contrast, a behaviour is rejected to the extent that it has the characteristics of a 'non-Parent', a 'stranger' as the French philosopher Camus would claim.

The values of an individual come from the past. The tools that are used in this book are not intended to change values – that would be pompous and time consuming – but to show that the behaviours being promoted are compatible with those that the individual already holds. To achieve this, there are two means:

1. *Putting people into the situation* by bringing them closer to the project (for example, site visits, role plays, seminars on pilot sites, and so on).
2. *The testimonies of highly regarded people*, that is those taken from the Parents' camp (the union representative, the well known scientist, and so on) rather than from the non-Parents' camp. Often, this simple contact is enough to provoke a change of attitude towards the project.

By contrast, it is often necessary to remove those who have a negative effect on the project. For example, directors who refuse to have computers on their desks will find it difficult to impose them on their subordinates. These principles have been applied to the insurance case.

A Lateral Project: the Level-IV Writers' Case

For this exercise, the authors' suggestions were sorted into Values/Usefulness/Desires as summarised in Figure 9.4.

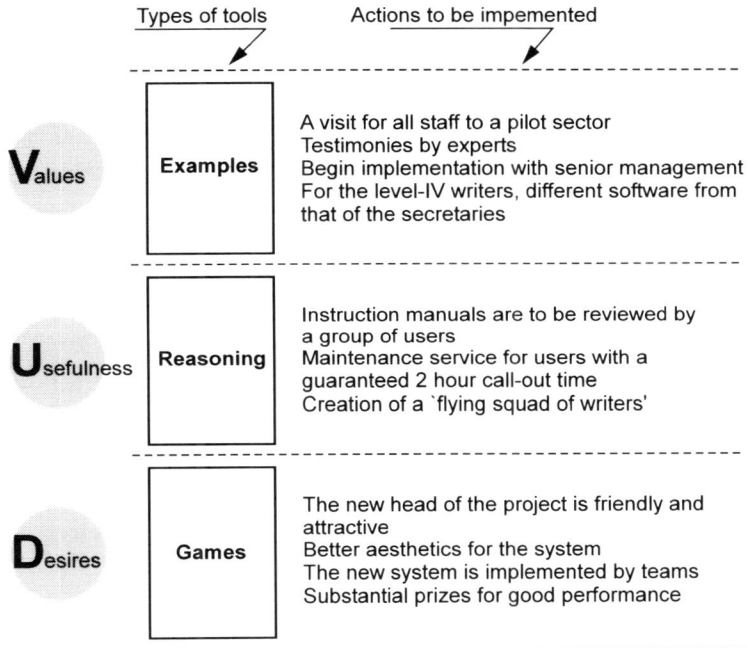

Figure 9.4 An example of how the project is enriched for the level-IV writer

In fact each of these suggestions carries several levels of meaning. To endow the project with values, the following actions were proposed:

- Launch a project titled 'Skills for the level-IV writer in the year 2000' with testimonies of approval from experts from several countries. This would be initiated with a small internal conference prepared by working groups composed of level-IV writers and members of the management team.
- Have all relevant staff visit a similar company equipped with a similar computing system: visits would be organised in groups of five without a management presence. This sensible proposal was opposed by the IT Director who feared his competence would be questioned (he wanted to emphasise the fact that the proposed system was more advanced than that of the competition).

- Have the project presented by the most competent allies among the writers.
- Start implementing the project with the installation of a pilot unit in the department director's office (this required negotiations lasting several weeks). Once the system was installed the director discovered faults in it, something that he had previously asserted as being impossible.
- Create software and special functions in the computer specifically for level-IV writers, called 'Mega 8'. This software was much more powerful and attractive than that of the secretaries, it allowed access to classified information and the screen was in colour. A specific desk for level-IV writers was to be installed at the same time as the computing system which allowed them to work differently (this proposal was very difficult to get accepted as it ran counter to the plan for a unique computer system).

To endow the project with usefulness for the writers, the following actions were proposed:

- Create a group of users to review the instruction manuals to make them more appropriate to the work.
- Have a maintenance service for users, with a guaranteed two-hour call-out time (the IT director did not agree with this service since he had guaranteed a breakdown ratio less than 2%, which made this service redundant). The breakdown rates actually experienced by users reached 14% in some weeks.
- The creation of a 'flying squad' of writers who were not attached to any groups but who could come to the rescue of any team facing an exceptional workload during the implementation of the project.

To endow the project with desires, the following actions were proposed:

- Replace the head of the project (on promotion), although he had been perfectly efficient in the preceding phases. That allowed:
  o a scapegoat to be blamed for mistakes so allowing the top management to save face, and
  o the introduction of a friendly and well-respected woman as head of the project. Her technical skills, without being bad, were not of the same standard as those of her predecessor, but she had the advantage of not turning every meeting into a pitched battle.

- Install improved software and aesthetically pleasing computers (as previously mentioned).
- Carry out the implementation by teamwork which allowed:
  - the creation of a friendly forum, the team meetings,
  - the introduction of competition by listing the results of teams, and
  - a substantial prize for the most successful implementers (a week for two in Barbados).

Evaluation

As can be seen, the Value/Usefulness/Desire grid allowed concrete measures to be taken. In particular it allows an understanding of the fact that bears are attracted by honey, not vinegar. So during World War II why did Churchill say: 'I have nothing to offer but blood, toil, tears and sweat'? This must not be interpreted as an attempt to motivate, but as a technique to 'clear the mines', which paved the way for a credible and attractive project: 'to win the war'.

Of particular note is the fact that most of the measures proposed were not words, but actions. To devise a lateral project is not only to find the right words, it is to develop the project and its emotional universe. (See Figure 9.5.)

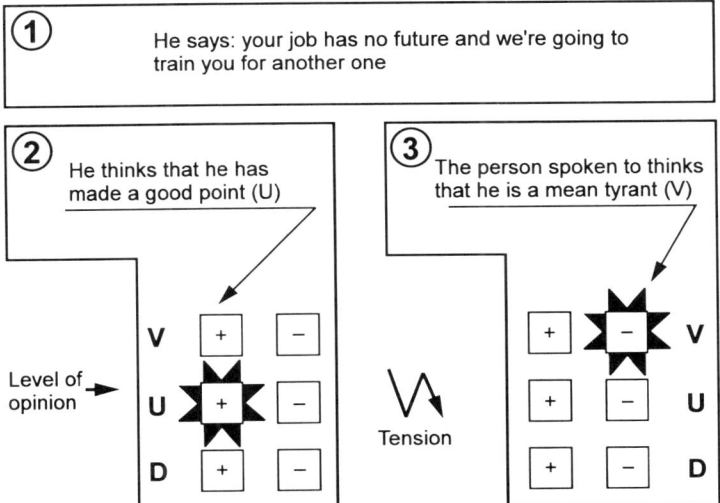

Figure 9.5 The mechanism of misunderstanding

POINTS TO REMEMBER

- What players accept only with great difficulty, and particularly the initiator of a project, are all attempts to get into the other's rationality.
- The VUD model attempts to represent the opinions of each person about the project according to three levels of perception that are different and complementary: Values, Usefulness and Desires.
  - the values of individuals are all those unconscious norms and rules which they obey without being aware of them;
  - the usefulness to the individuals are all the opinions they are conscious of – usefulness is by definition rational and thus negotiable;
  - the desires of the individual are the most hidden; desire is the engine while the norm is the steering wheel.
- To rewrite the project and transform it into a lateral project, a way must be found to occupy these three levels of perception.
- To devise a lateral project is not just to find the right words, it is to develop the project and its emotional universe.

10 Do Not Respect Time, Respect Timing

The second most important aspect in the definition of a lateral project is the choice of the pace at which the change is to be made: its link with time. The resisting forces the authors have encountered in sensitive projects are extraordinary for many reasons. If people are ready to accept a certain change in their lives or if they have a certain amount of flexibility, this flexibility has limits which are quickly reached.

Hubert Reeves, the celebrated astrophysicist from Montreal University, writes that Einstein created a revolution by discovering relativity between 1905 and 1925, but showed himself to be narrow-minded thereafter, to the point of being incapable of accepting new developments in quantum physics being advanced by other theorists.

People are not ready to change much. Sometimes, even, they might want to change but fail to do so. Anyone who has tried to lose weight or to quit smoking will understand this. There are limits to desires, and these limits are values (this phrase is considered as the definition of the word value). A strong emphasis has been placed on desires in the last chapter, but now the focus is on values.

If a project is sensitive, it is often because it overstretches the natural flexibility of the individual. It requires a behavioural change or a break from what is currently accepted. Many believe that time alone will allow the values of players to change. How long will this change take? This is a matter of strategy because there is a choice: to advance quickly, to go more slowly, even to stop: this choice is an important element in defining a lateral project.

INDIVIDUALS DO NOT NEED TIME TO CHANGE, THEY NEED A STRUCTURE, A CREDIBLE 'WAY OUT'

The capacity to change the behaviours of individuals is limited by their normative systems, what is called their 'built-in justification':

- built-in because from individuals' utterances it is possible to note the way their desires and values are structured; for example, individuals

are capable of explaining to a certain extent why they are for or against the death penalty;
- justification because it is quickly perceived that there is a very strong link between the opinions expressed and the ideas people have of themselves, that is, the justification they give to the fact that they are who they are.

The built-in justification is a system which allows individuals to explain to themselves their existence and to give them reasons to be content with it. This explanation need not be scientific (it could not be anyway). It must be structured, that is it must be able to resist questioning assaults. In ancient times myths explained natural and human phenomena in a sufficiently satisfactory way for people to be content with them for thousands of years. Today some myths still survive. The difference between the myth and the built-in justification is that the former is collective while the latter is individualistic.

Built-in justification is like a building whose weight is distributed on walls that are themselves resting on foundations. If a new window is needed, the existing forces must be calculated and then supporting beams must be installed before the wall is opened up; otherwise there is a risk the whole building will collapse.

This explains the importance of the notion of a 'way out' so noticeable in Japanese civilisation. In that culture, it is explicitly admitted a person must not be made to lose face. *This simply means that people must be given a good reason to lose, a reason which allows them to continue to look themselves in the face and then to face the glances of others.*

When changes are made to organisations, or processes made more cost-effective, this can – without the management being aware of it – have the effect of treading on people's reasons for living. Then, social forces are released which totally outweigh the original project. The way out for those concerned is to revolt. It is not the worst that can happen, since revolt is a form of energy, and energy can be focused. The worst is collapse.

Today, there is much debate about the homeless, many of whom find themselves on the streets because of unemployment. Their predicament is due – it is thought – to a lack of resources. Many are ready to help them financially. But those whose task it is to find them homes face a problem more terrifying than a lack of resources: the lack of desires and of values. Their built-in justification has been shattered and there is nothing to support them to bring them back into society. Care homes remain half empty, because some homeless cannot tolerate the discipline that is

An Acceptable Way Out: Rita's Case

In a care organisation, a middle-aged employee Rita has become the director's secretary. This position entitles her to occupy the office next to his. The organisation is undergoing a vast review of its activities which clearly indicates that the position of director's secretary is redundant. The newly-created position of administrative manager is offered to Rita. In this organisation compulsory lay-offs are virtually impossible. The more so for Rita since she is fifty years old and her quite high salary, given her qualifications, makes any hope of redeployment difficult within the company.

Against all expectations, Rita prefers to resign rather than lose her position as the director's secretary and her office next to his. In so doing she abandons her salary and her job security. However, during the negotiations to implement the new organisational structure everything was done to try to satisfy her. Her director's secretary title would be maintained, a bonus is awarded to her for the change of position and she is given the opportunity to choose her new office.

Evaluation

On analysis it seems that for Rita, a straightforward person, the fact that she was in the office next to the director's was her reason for living: that justified, in her eyes, her standing among the rest of the staff and her mother's pride, whose only compensation for a difficult life was her daughter's success.

Rita preferred to resign because that allowed her not to change her built-in justification: she could blame her departure on the newly-appointed and politically manipulative director who wished to promote a young person of his acquaintance. Her mother, an old socialist, would accept this explanation more readily than a change of status. So Rita quit her job by resigning.

Her case is certainly a failure. But in human terms it is not a failure. Unconsciously, Rita finds a way out. Even if it is shocking the result of this operation is win/win. The management is satisfied and she is satisfied.

imposed on the residents. They are totally devoid of structure, their built-in justification has imploded. Work structured their lives. Without work, they no longer have a structure.

With a sensitive project, *the objective is not necessarily to convince people but systematically to find a way out* for those whose life is going to change, otherwise there will be distressing social outbursts.

THE TIME NEEDED TO GET GOOD ACCEPTANCE FOR A PROJECT IS ONLY LINKED TO THE CAPACITY TO HELP PEOPLE REBUILD THEMSELVES

In sensitive projects, sometimes the first reaction is to give people time so that they can get used to the new realities. This is pointless. If it were enough to give extra time for individuals to get used to change, the homeless would not remain on the streets for very long. However, if nothing is done they will remain homeless forever.

A director of a computer training centre of world repute has shown that a generation of programmers could not get used to the new ways of programming, despite the time and the energy spent on training. This is his story:

The Cobol Case: A Lateral Project of Object Programming

The work of computer programmers has been revolutionised by the arrival of a new method of programming: 'object programming', which leads to considerable time savings. This has begun to replace an older technique, Cobol programming, familiar to all those who studied computing. Even now most classical computer programmers use Cobol. Object programming and Cobol are as diametrically opposed as night and day.

A software publisher, Microfocus, launches a new product whose name is shocking: the 'Cobol Object'. To a purist, Cobol cannot be an Object. The gurus of the object approach greet the announcement of the Microfocus product with complete derision. This is not a surprise, but it is a complete mistake. The evidence is there for everyone to see: despite some definite progress on standardisation and benefits, the object approach to management software has yet to take off. There are practical difficulties, as reported by those companies engaged in large-scale implementation of the object approach.

Experience also shows that training takes longer, it is more costly and intellectually more demanding than expected. Taking into account the initial training, monitoring, re-training and re-monitoring, the conversion of a Cobol programmer into an object programmer is rarely completed in less than six months. Sometimes this painful process of unlearning traditional programming logic takes over a year before the object mode of thinking is absorbed. For Cobolists this cultural gap is impossible to bridge.

More subtly, there are other forces resisting the object approach, not least project leaders and training professionals. This is understandable: to forecast, plan, control and monitor the progress of traditional projects is already a difficult task. But to take on the object approach – without guidance or benchmarks, when the process is by its very nature iterative (sometimes with iterations that are long indeed) – is a challenge for only the bravest of managers.

The object approach, as it name suggest, is about sharing objects between those who created them and those who are going to use them. Actually, this ends up being rather laborious as soon as the project is rolled out from the project team into the whole company. Now it is not a question of object or no object – it is no longer a question of skills, but a question of organisation, of discipline and of political will. This almost brings the project back to the very beginning.

In other words, despite some considerable advantages even its most ardent allies cannot deny that the object approach has not won the battle. A future Cobol Object could be very useful, no matter how distressing this is for the purists. Of course they are right, these purists, the object logic and the Cobol logic are incompatible, and even fundamentally contradictory. Of course, to move from one to the other, the Cobol programmers will have to make a difficult transition to a new way of thinking. But with Cobol Object this would at least happen using a familiar syntax. The battle will not be won because of that, but experience shows that in computing as for everything else, it is easier to succeed with evolution rather than revolution.

Evaluation

This shows that the computing world has not found a way of rebuilding computer programmers, despite the time and concepts. This will undoubtedly please those technophobes who have had to endure the mocking of that technologically advanced profession. The Cobol Object is, however, the epitome of a clever lateral project.

GETTING THE TIMING RIGHT

Those sensitive projects which are a hit, as they say in show business, often succeed through a series of lateral projects which, little by little, lead to the final objective. Why is it that some new values settle in without difficulty while others provoke immediate rejections? Let's take the example of the deregulation of the post office and the telecommunications business.

A Revolution without Trouble: Splitting the French Post Office and Telecommunications Services

For over ten years there has been a project to split the French PTT into a separate post office and telecommunications service. This has been advancing systematically, despite changes in governments and management. Many analysts believe it will take another ten years to achieve the total plan.

In 1982, when the managing director of the telecommunications side started this process, no one – from any side of the political spectrum – thought it possible. Today, however, the two companies have a separate legal structure, distinct buildings, independent recruitment and, this says it all, distinct futures. All that remains to be done is to change the status of employees. Time did its work. Inexorably, people got used to it, behaviours adapted and the change progressed.

Evaluation

The choice which was made by the PTT in 1982 seemed to be the most appropriate. It played on values rather than reason, starting with a strong value: the name of the company. In 1986 the PTT became two entities: the Post Office on one side and French Telecom on the other. Of course, the required legal structure followed suit, but the name existed before the legal structure. Bit by bit, the PTT vanished from the language among customers as well as staff.

Expressing the project through successive layers, using successive lateral projects, can contribute to its success (see Figure 10.1). The technique of the lateral project is to agree a credible formulation in the short term, while leaving the door open for other more ambitious

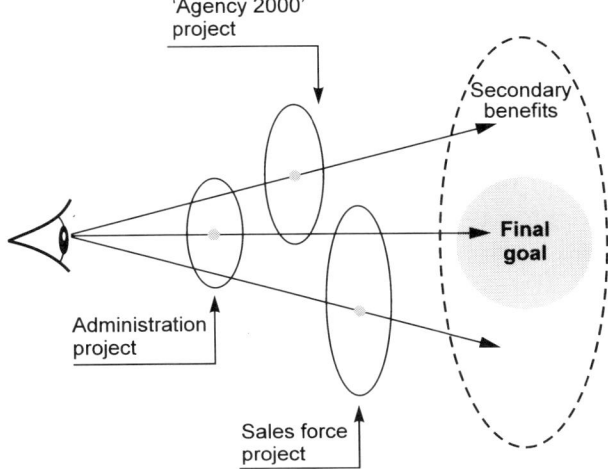

Figure 10.1 A number of lateral projects may be needed in order to ensure that an ambitious goal is achieved

evolutions which cannot be understood at the moment. This ability to segment the progress of the project into concrete and acceptable steps requires both courage and imagination.

Experts in neuro-linguistic programming speak of *synchronisation* to describe the necessary attuning of players before a meaningful communication can be envisaged. Anthony Robbins, the famous American author of self-help books, says that before leading people, we must first follow them, that is to say, show them that we are alike, repeat their gestures, speech, ideas, behaviour and dress code. At a given time, you reach a stage where you can introduce some changes, a stage where the affinity is such that when you transform your behaviour, they will follow suit.

This intermediate phase where one adapts one's speech and behaviour to that of others is not strictly speaking a communication phase: nothing new is being said. We show that we belong to the same world, that we understand the other. This is what we call a synchronisation phase.

One phase of the mediation–revelation process – the clearing of mines – is a synchronisation phase. For example, the authors have often found structural problems of synchronisation with clients. In the first few days the client presents the problem, and everyone agrees on the way to remedy this. Then the consultants start to work. Meantime the client gets on with business as usual dealing with a thousand and one issues. The consultants are totally focused on the problem to be solved. At the progress meeting, if care is not taken, a problem of synchronisation is bound to crop up. The consultants are completely immersed in the subject and eager to speak of solutions, when the client is left at the beginning with the original presentation of the problem. A substantial part of the meeting – even if time is pressing – must be spent on guiding the client through developments since the first meeting.

Many sensitive projects are confronted with this difficulty. A proposal is put forward. It is immediately rejected by someone as being stupid, not practical, unsuitable, even preposterous. Then the proposer decides to do something else and abandons that solution. The person who rejected it begins to reconsider, discusses the matter with others, and step by step understands the benefits to be had. They meet again. But it is too late: the game is over. Another solution, probably less cost-effective, has been found: the two people lacked synchronisation.

If synchronisation is important, it is not sufficient. A lateral project cannot be a simple synchronisation, it is the expression at a given moment of a change that is thought acceptable to the allies.

SIX TECHNIQUES FOR 'RESYNCHRONISING' ONESELF WITH PLAYERS – STARTING OFF ON THE RIGHT FOOT

All this might seem a bit theoretical to someone who is facing 10 000 people on the streets asking for his or her dismissal. Very practically, how does one synchronise with players when it is obvious that this does not exist currently? The ideal would be to stop and to take time to find this synchronisation. But is it possible to do it? A herd of charging elephants cannot be stopped.

Six techniques are commonly used:

- *The break.* The game is stopped to agree on a method to move forward. This is the simplest case: a project was launched and was widely resisted causing uproar. Hence the principle of the break – as in basketball – proposes the suspension of the project: it was due to start in September, but its implementation is postponed until September of the following year. The time will be used to meet everyone and to get agreement. The project is not cancelled, it is postponed to take the pressure off and to win time to convince others.

- *Kick into touch.* This is a technique used in rugby when the pressure from the opposing team is strong and the ball is kicked out of play. The idea is the same as the break but the principle is the reverse: an ambitious objective is set but it is planned for a long time in the future. This is what happened with the plans for a single European currency. The objective – which today looks unrealistic – was at first set for June 1998, then 1999. The decision becomes less insurmountable but it has been made. The objective of kicking into touch is to occupy the ground until the game resumes. The decision becomes so obvious that with the passage of time people get accustomed to it. To do this, one must not just wait, one must occupy the ground.
- *Arbitration.* Arbitration is a sophisticated break. It gives a third party the task of giving an opinion on the conditions for the implementation of the project. In modern democracies, the state is familiar with sensitive projects and a system has been developed to make everything more transparent. Sometimes, this is referred to as open government. In practice a report or a series of reports – sometimes called Green Papers – are produced for discussion and consultation.

    These reports first consider all the problems, and then propose solutions. For example, governments can have papers produced on sensitive topics such as the health service, financing further education or pensions in the next century.

    The author of the report is not asked to give expert advice but to give recommendations on what it is possible to envisage taking into account the agendas of the various players. To compile the report these players are met, or they make written submissions and their suggestions are considered. After this round of meetings the report is written and presented to government. Depending on the reactions the report elicits, the government has some freedom on what to do next. The report can be buried, published, debated in parliament or become the basis of a law. Whatever happens, the report will have helped the synchronisation of the players.
- *Create a test site.* There is an advantage in having a location to show for the future communication of a project. This helps prove that the assumptions on which the project is based are well-founded and, more importantly, it enables people to put themselves into the situation. The creation of a test site is easy as it only concerns a minority of people, chosen of course from amongst the allies of the project. The time to create this site and to make it function is very beneficial for further work on the ground.

- *Call for volunteers.* The amount of time and energy spent by project leaders trying to impose projects on communities, workers or people never fails to surprise the authors. By far the simplest way forward is to ask for volunteers (particularly for the creation of a pilot site). Of course, one has to make the proposal attractive by adding to it some benefits. But experience shows that volunteers will arise from the process. Moreover, these volunteers are better allies than anyone who might have the project imposed on them.
- *Call for contributions/hand the problem to someone else.* The call for contributions applies to projects where the volunteer process is not possible. It is based on the well-known principle that everyone agrees on problems but not on solutions. The idea is to highlight the problem and ask the players to propose solutions, then help the players experiment with the solutions they have proposed.

Caution does not consist of slowing down change. Caution consists of constantly making sure that the change is understood.

POINTS TO REMEMBER

- Built-in justification is a system which allows individuals to explain to themselves why they exist and to give them reasons to be content with it.
- The objective is not to convince, but systematically to find a way for players to preserve their built-in justification.
- That does not necessarily require time, but rather an effort in synchronisation. There are six techniques to resynchronise the players.
- To give time to time is too often a way of losing it.
- The lateral project might just be a short-term step, leaving the door open for more ambitious evolutions that are too difficult to get agreement on at present.

11 Going for Broke

When devising a lateral project there is always the risk – in the search for consensus – of ending up with a manipulated formula, devoid of sense, which gets rid of all the difficulties and kills with kindness. The lateral projects one might end up with – if one is not careful – resemble in a strange way knives without blades, or handles either. In the end nothing has changed or the changes have been so minuscule as to make one wonder what all the fuss was about.

It is the opposite which must be done. If a project provokes tensions, then these tensions must express themselves. It is not by making the project more vague that it will become more accessible. The objective is not to avoid tensions, but to make understood what the players do not necessarily understand. It is not by asserting that nothing will change that a better result is obtained. One must go for broke by announcing that things are going to change, possibly even radically. It is not the principle of change which will heighten tension, it is the way it is expressed.

FIND NEW WORDS WHICH ARE NOT CONNECTED TO THE PAST AND WHICH DESCRIBE WHAT IS ABOUT TO BE DONE IN CONCRETE TERMS

As noted, words mean different things to different people. This difference exists at a *denotative level*, that is, in the first sense of the word.

A Misunderstanding between Accountants and Sales Representatives

Accountants refer to clients as third parties and use the same word to describe suppliers, as well as anyone who is not an employee of the firm or a shareholder. Representatives call clients 'customers'. A bank is planning to install an IT project for its salesforce. This project is called the Third Party Database Project because it was devised by accountants. However, to the sales representatives:

> - the word database does not mean anything (the only base they know might be the 'airforce base'); and
> - third party means 'somebody other than the customer'. The representative segments the world into three parts: us (the bank), the customers (who might also be prospects), and third parties (all the rest).
>
> If the company wants to introduce this system for representatives, it would be better called: 'The Universal Customer Filing System Project' even if it is not a filing system, and if it also includes prospects as well as customers.

This difference in the understanding of words also exists for the *connotative meaning*, that is the personal meaning that is attributed to words and which results from people's own backgrounds. To call a computer Apple would be more attractive to some people than to call it IBM or COMPAQ. To others, it could be the contrary. In a pharmaceutical company to call a representative a 'sales executive' would be simply impossible. On the other hand, 'adviser' or 'consultant' might be tolerated.

Words are part of the values that structure the built-in justification of individuals. Each individual uses his or her own words to describe the world. To use other words is to risk appearing as 'the stranger'. But this is also the time to make people understand that the project is different from what they have known previously.

When learning to paint, an art teacher shows how to create the green of the trees and the undergrowth in the light of the sun. From that day, trees will never be seen in the same way. They are perceived in colour in a way they have never been seen before.

Similarly, if sociodynamics is used to describe the relationships between people, these relationships will never be seen in the same way again. Once one becomes aware of the term passives, suddenly the world becomes filled with them, where before there was a butcher, a head of department or an uncle.

There Cannot be Change without a Breakdown

Psychologists say: to change we must bury the past. To bury an organisation, new words must also be created to replace the old ones. Two conclusions emerge:

1. *To truly change, new words must be used.* It is difficult to change people if the words which describe things do not change. How can it be made clear that one is revolutionising the Out Patients' Department if it is still called the Out Patients' Department?

This is also a good method of testing whether an individual is beginning to enter into the change process. One analyses whether old words (for example, head of personnel) or new words (human resources department) are being used.

2. *Better still, one must encourage the players to create and use new words.* To change the responsibilities and behaviour of supervisors in a factory, the new role should be presented and suggestions sought as to the title which would fit the new position. By discussing names, they understand what is expected of them. The day this new name is used by them and their subordinates, is the day the reform has succeeded.

Nowadays, companies throw themselves wholeheartedly into certification projects; that strangely resemble administrative programmes; that is to say, write what is to be done, and do it. But these days 'administrative procedure' projects will have no chance of success as they sound boring, while 'certification' projects are embraced with enthusiasm. Among the new words, those words describing organisations are particularly important.

**New Words to Explain New Things:
The Case of the French Post Office**

The French Post Office, an organisation with 380 000 employees, does not want to be only a company made up of postmen and postwomen delivering letters. It also wants to become a sales network, possibly one of the most important in France, capable of providing not only mail services but also financial services, like a bank. It is still a long way from achieving this goal. However, in advance of this change the Post Office has radically modified its organisation by segmenting staff into three departments: two departments supplying 'products', the mailing department and the financial services department; and a network department which distributes the products made by the other two. As such, each of the employees of the Post Office has to be able to know whether they are manufacturers, bankers or distributors.

This capacity to propose a new architecture for an organisation is one of the key points in defining an efficient lateral project. Modern architecture can be blamed for having disorganised our living space. When one looks at some buildings it is difficult to know where the doors and the windows are. City maps have also become very difficult to understand; it is hard to pinpoint the centre or to find where the shops are. We simply cannot find our way. Some experts claim this destructured architecture leads to a sense of isolation which, in turn, leads to increased tension and violence in some areas.

In the same way some companies, following rapid growth, have devised an organisational structure so incomprehensible that those who work within it have difficulty understanding it, not to mention those who have to interpret it from the outside. It is not surprising that this disordered architecture creates tensions where there should be none. To identify clearly who is responsible for what, is not only the clarification of roles and functions it is also bringing about an understanding of what the company is, what its purpose is and how it functions.

AVOID IMPERCEPTIBLE CHANGE

Faced with a difficult change, a manager vacillates between being audacious and cautious. How far can he or she go? The authors are rather in favour of being audacious. Everyone is aware of the need for caution, but paradoxically if decisions are watered down they become unintelligible. Quite naturally individuals tend to revert to their past behaviours as they are familiar with them. To fudge the moment of change provides another opportunity for these old habits to reassert themselves.

If one has to choose between numerous small changes over a period of time or one big change at a given moment, the latter is favoured for five key reasons:

- *Savings.* To make numerous small changes costs, psychologically, many times the price of a big change.
- *Visibility for the players.* When there are many changes people tend to lose track of where they are. In contrast, if everyone moves to a new system at a fixed point in time, everyone knows exactly when the change is in place.
- *Making the change sacrosanct.* If the day of change is fixed in the calendar it is psychologically much more difficult to postpone it – even for a few hours.

- *Systemic functioning.* The change is registered as part of a collective process. It is more difficult for individuals to change if their total environment does not change at the same time.
- *The ratchet effect.* After the moment of change the impression is given that it is impossible to turn back.

So, the lateral project does not hide the change by pretending that everything is going to stay the same: on the contrary it makes the change more desirable. Everything then is a question of adjustment.

POINTS TO REMEMBER

- It is not by making a project vague that it is made more accessible.
- To really change, new words must be used.
- Better still, the players must be encouraged to create the new words and use them.
- If one can choose between numerous small changes spread over time and a big change at a fixed time, the latter is preferred.
- A lateral project must appear as a break in advance of better times to come.

12 Have Allies Write the Lateral Project

The best lateral projects are those devised by allies. *Allies are in the best position to convince their peers.*

People will listen with greater attention to one of their own people whom they trust rather than someone they do not know and respect. People who are close to individuals and their problems are best placed to respond to them. There is no one better equipped to speak to the unions than a union representative, or a teacher to speak to teachers, and so on.

The power of allies rests on the fact that it is founded on a network of players who are close to the ground. Allies know how to couch the project in terms that best suit the players they represent. These allies will also know how to convince the project management to make modifications to render the project more presentable. As allies, they will find the words to tell management what they normally refuse to hear.

ALLIES ARE MORE CONVINCED IF THEY DISCOVER THE ARGUMENTS TO CONVINCE THEMSELVES

American researchers have uncovered a phenomenon they called cognitive dissonance, whose principle is as follows: people's opinions are consistent with their behaviours, as seen in the principle of built-in justification. A change of opinion will lead to a change of behaviour, but conversely a change of behaviour will inevitably lead to a change of opinion.

Several examples of cognitive dissonance are known. Robert Cialdini, the American psychologist and the author of *Influence*, quotes the case of door-to-door sales and the contracts people sign.

> ### A Case of Self-Suggestion: Door-to-Door Selling
>
> Many countries have passed laws to stop underhand sales techniques – such as intimidation and sharp practice – which force customers to buy goods, they do not really want. One law allows a cooling-off period, whereby the purchaser can cancel an agreement even if signed. When the law was introduced in the United States there were huge numbers of cancellations. But companies soon discovered a simple and perfectly legal technique which dramatically reduced the number of cancellations. The contract document was completed by the buyers not the salesperson. The training manual of one large door-to-door sales organisation said that this form of written agreement became 'an essential element to prevent customers from cancelling contracts'.
>
> **Evaluation**
>
> It is as if the buyers do not want to contradict themselves, but the authors are not convinced by Robert Cialdini's interpretation of this phenomenon. He supposes that it is the pressure exerted by others which provokes the change in behaviour. The authors contend that the others only act as a mirror for the individual. What they think is part of them. Their behaviours are them. Putting them face to face with a contradiction is to question the opinion they have of themselves and that is unacceptable.

By the same principle, to involve allies in the conception of a lateral project convinces them more certainly of its advantages than any arguments which are imposed on them.

EVERYTHING THAT IS SAID WILL, WITHOUT DOUBT, BE MARKED WITH A STRONG 'SOURCE EFFECT'

Statements vary in meaning according to who issues them – this is called the source effect. It is clear that if the leader of a local pressure group says to the residents: 'This project protects our interests', this will be better accepted than if a government minister promises the same thing.

In sensitive projects voices of authority are often not respected, because they defend general interests which are often at odds with the particular specific interests of the people listening. It is better to let allies express themselves rather than risk having the message damaged before it is even uttered. This principle applies particularly to the project initiators as they are rarely seen as credible players because:

- their behaviour was not blameless in the past. For example, how can one be credible in launching a new work practice, when each of the previous reforms led to redundancies?
- their impartiality is called into question. For example, on a motorway project the builder is also the company which benefits financially.

The key indicator that a project has become truly lateral is when an ally adopts it.

POINTS TO REMEMBER

- Allies are better placed to convince those who have similarities with them.
- Allies are all the more convinced if they themselves find the arguments which convince them.
- Everything that is said will inevitably be marked with a strong source effect.
- The lateral project only has real meaning when it is advocated by an ally.

13 Moving from Penalties to Benefits

SANCTIONS AND ANTAGONISM

The last important aspect to understand about a lateral project is its content in terms of sanctions. Unlike ordinary projects, sensitive projects are characterised by their appeal to morals. There is talk of honesty and dishonesty, faults, responsibility, courage, duplicity and, of course, penalties. When those who have initiated a project are suddenly stopped in their tracks, the first instinct is to use power. The concept of punishment is ever present. For example:

- a developer decides not to support a local charity's fund-raising day, because one of the committee members spoke out against the project; or
- a sales director decides to give lower pay rises to those members of the team who resisted the introduction of computerisation.

These attitudes engender the reverse behaviour: rebellion. The punishment is punished in turn. Antagonism generates antagonism. For example:

- the member of the charity committee is the brother of a local councillor who organises a motion of opposition against the developer's new housing scheme – just before it goes before the planning committee;
- the salesmen begin to 'lose' their computers which have to replaced at some expense by the company.

Why is it that what is normally accepted (a new road is badly needed, for example) becomes a source of conflict in a sensitive project? A long time ago, the French legislator, Montesquieu, answered this with the principle that power must be segmented: it is fundamental to separate those who make the rules from those who apply the penalties. What happens if this is not so? Whoever applies the sanctions appears as judge and judged at the same time, and this is perceived as unjust.

This phenomenon – a classic of social functioning – is particularly delicate in the case of sensitive projects. In effect, if a project is sensitive it is precisely so because it changes values and norms which are common and well-entrenched. The use of sanctions becomes all the more delicate as the individual refuses to accept the basic principle.

There is general agreement that a professional bank robber should be put into jail. But if the same action is taken by a freedom fighter during war-time it might appear heroic. Now the punishment which seems natural would appear unjust if it were applied in war-time by enemy forces.

Those responsible for sensitive projects find it difficult to understand that they appear as 'those who make the laws'. A judge will find it difficult to convince a young thief that stealing cars is a reprehensible act. The boy does not have the same reference frame as the judge. For him, the judge, like the teacher and the boss who refuses to employ him, are people benefiting from a system which is hostile to him as a matter of principle, whether he steals a car or not. The law they apply is their law not his. So, to get the young man on the right track, he must be asked to define his law, the law he would like somebody to apply to him, then it will be applied to him. What is learnt from this boy, we must also apply to the elderly salesman whose built-in justification is being shattered.

REWARDS

It is therefore pointless to apply laws that no one respects! The head of a project must, before all else, *respect the process of creating values*. Then these become benchmarks which can be referred to. The lateral project must be devised so *as not to put sanctions in place which cannot be applied*, but to respect the process of creating values. Three principles of action are useful:

- The first is positive sanctioning, that is to reward those who participate in the project. So, if in a group of 100 salesmen ten categorically refuse a new organisation system and 10 actively support it, one would try to give a bonus to those who succeed, rather than a warning to those who failed (allies' strategy). This is not, however, the most common reaction.
- The second principle consists of asking the group to define the rewards and sanctions in the case of success and failure. The debate can be rough, but experience shows that this discussion allows a true

synchronisation with the players. Discussing sanctions and rewards makes the objectives clear. It leads the players themselves to apply the rewards and penalties.
- The best principle involves, not sanctions, but the concept of benefits expected from the project. Without trying to say what is good or bad, the benefit that the community would get from a project, if it succeeds, are put forward. If the lateral project has been correctly devised, there must be an effective benefit obvious to all.

POINTS TO REMEMBER

- Antagonism generates antagonism.
- Those responsible for sensitive projects find it difficult to understand that they appear as 'those who make the law'. They cannot impose what they have devised without appearing as judge and judged, which is seen as unjust.
- A project is sensitive precisely because there are no norms accepted by all. So, punishment no longer carries the same value: it is not punishment, it is tyranny.
- A lateral project must enhance expected benefits rather than penalties which would be applied in the case of refusal or failure.

Part IV
Developing the Dynamics of the Lateral Project

Metaphorically speaking, the outcome of the first three parts of this book has been that the ship has managed to leave harbour, notwithstanding the bad weather. First, the situation was analysed with the help of the concepts outlined in Part I. The project was launched following the principles described in Part II, that is by mobilising the first circle of allies on a lateral project. There is now a lateral project which, if the principles detailed in Part III have been followed, is devised in such a way as to maximise the field of allies. Next is the navigation phase.

One might believe that with a good project, and with some allies determined to see it succeed, most of the work has been done. Curiously, it is in this navigation phase that the most unpleasant surprises are encountered. If, and let's not be deluded, the project is sensitive it is because it carries two characteristics that will remain with it until it is completed:

1. *It is complex* – the players themselves do not understand all its far-reaching implications. The modalities of the project will become clearer in the implementation phase. So there will have to be explanations, further explanations and then more explanations.
2. *There is no unanimous agreement* – opposition creates stress among the players, whether they are allies or opponents, which leads them to adopt unreasonable behaviours.

The launch generally happens without too much trouble because everyone fears a noisy outburst and so care is taken. But as soon as things seem to be on track, the methodology begins to slip and difficulties appear, beginning with dissension among allies. Soon, everyone reverts to the magpie syndrome: fire-fighting incidents with opponents instead of maintaining allies. Care is not taken of the factors which motivate the allies. The project leaders start to give them orders, and at the same time their energy fades away as the tension reduces.

The success of a sensitive project is like a marathon. It is achieved day by day, with constant attention to what motivates the players. This is why the strategy for a lateral project cannot be viewed as an expeditious remedy for specific tensions. It is not a one-off quick fix. It is a universal principle of managing sensitive projects from the beginning to completion.

How can the collective dynamic of allies be maintained and developed around a lateral project? Energy and resources must be expended to achieve three objectives:

1. *Help allies attain the objectives that they have set themselves.* Difficult or not, a project is a project: it is firstly work, time passing, deadlines that are postponed and budgets that are soaring. To help the allies, those who are concretely building the project, is therefore vital. This is not necessarily simple.
2. *Know, on a day-by-day basis, reactions on the ground* and adapt actions accordingly. Every action is going to influence the opinion of the players one wants to convince. Attention must be paid to all these micro-facts, to check that they do not give a misleading impression of the project and, if they do, to correct them systematically.
3. *Ensure the unity of those responsible.* This will avoid dissension in the project management camp.

14 Helping Allies to Act

Actions by allies are indispensable: it is they who will 'make' the project in real terms. Once the first circle is formed, and once it is working, two types of behaviours should be avoided by the project management:

- *Leaving the allies on their own.* Leaving the allies to act totally on their own runs the risk that they will stop at the first difficulty, or, worse, that they might lose track of what is to be achieved. The first circle of allies is constructed to ensure it is composed of people who take initiatives; that is why they were chosen in the first place. However, if they sense that they are not being followed up and sustained, they may become discouraged. *The level of autonomy of these players is weak –* from a few hours to a month in the best cases. Therefore they must be 're-primed' at least every month, and more likely every week or two.
- *Acting for them.* If allies are poor at organising themselves or acting, it is tempting to tell them what to do or even for project members to do it themselves. In fact the allies' real problem is in doing things. How many allies support a project but do nothing? They speak, they applaud, they give words of encouragement but they don't go on the stage: they remain spectators. By telling them what to do, by replacing them, there are two risks: first, it increases their antagonism, which is what happens when a point of view is imposed on someone who does not agree; and, second, preventing their ownership of the project means the failure of the strategy of the lateral project.

What can be done to make people act? How can allies' synergy be developed without increasing their antagonism? How can we put them into play without finding the project in the firing line? A *help relationship* must be developed.

THE DIFFICULTY WITH HELPING

Managers without children are at a disadvantage compared to those with families. When childless managers see that their subordinates are not following orders, they might assume they are stupid. A father whose child does not manage to do what is taught, despite encouragement and punishment, does not have a choice. His child could not possibly be stupid. So he has a natural tendency to listen to those who speak of teaching skills and of 'help' relationships.

It is not because we want to help somebody that we succeed. Take a simple example: learning to swim. It is certainly not by explaining to the child, every evening from 8.00 to 9.00, swimming movements that a parent will teach a child to swim independently. By giving such attention to the child the parent is only maintaining *a dependence relationship* which might become permanent. The child, delighted with the attention, will do everything to avoid learning to swim in order to get the same attention every evening.

If the same worn-out parent decides to give the child total autonomy to play computer games, rather than do homework, then the child's school results will be poor. Any teacher understands this: if the parent is not interested in what the child is doing, then the child will look elsewhere for signs of support. Therefore, the help relationship is very delicate to implement. Between dependency and self-help the right path must be found: *to help is not to replace*. Management literature is full of advice and recipes on this subject.

What distinguishes the help relationship in sensitive projects is, above all, the tension and the stress. The relationship that was so effortless when everything was going well becomes difficult. The other party is not listening anymore. Worse, he or she might turn against someone who failed to help.

ESTABLISHING AN EFFICIENT HELP RELATIONSHIP

Carl Rogers, the American psychologist, identified necessary conditions for an efficient help relationship. Let's focus on four of them:

1. *Do not help someone who does not ask for help.* This is both a consequence of sociodynamics and a life principle which saves a lot of time, a great deal of perspiration and which, at the same time, respects the players. There is no point in telling allies, if they vacillate, what to do. One must wait until they ask for advice. That does not mean that one must stay motionless. There is nothing stopping one

from 'popping by to say hello'. But recommendations must not be made. The mere fact of being there will already be a great help. Some well-thought-out questions will surely give a hint of the more concrete help that could be available.

Asking for help must be considered as a synergetic attitude. It is an initiative. To help those who take initiatives is to apply the allies' strategy. To help someone who does not ask for help is to run the risk of expending energy on an opponent or a passive.

2. *Adopt an open attitude.* Carl Rogers was the first to undertake scientific studies to evaluate the most 'helping' behaviours, that is to say, those which allow those helped to make progress by themselves. He has shown that two behaviours were particularly efficient and formed what he termed an open attitude:

- First, *empathy,* which demonstrates that one perceives what the other party feels and that one understands the other party. This shows itself in the fact that one is capable of reformulating what the other has said in an appropriate fashion. It is essential to repeat to a person what he or she has just said before proposing an explanation or a ready-made model. This attitude of empathy allows synchronisation. Rather than say to a manager who fails to organise staff for a meeting to present a new project: 'You are the only one who has not organised the meeting', one could say: 'You have a particularly difficult team, I understand your caution: how do you propose to deal with this?'
- Second, *positive feelings,* what Rogers calls 'unconditional positive considerations', manifested towards the other party. For example, one may say, 'Whatever happens, I'll be there' or 'I am on your side, even if I am not always in agreement with you'. One would not say, as has recently been heard from the CEO of a major corporation: 'I am not responding to this question, it is stupid'. It is best to avoid the attitudes of the technocrats which tend to lead to 'looking coldly at the situation'. On the contrary, one should try to look at the situation warmly and together, taking people as we find them and accepting their differences. Successes, however small, are shared with enthusiasm and one sympathises with the failures, even if these are great.

It is worth remarking that what seems obvious when written in a book, becomes extremely difficult to implement when one is faced with the reality of a tense situation. There are several means to ensure the project team's open attitude:

- make one-to-one contact and take the opportunity after the interview to discuss the quality of the relationship;
- have regular 'synthesis' meetings for project team members which are exclusively dedicated to evaluating the quality of the personal relationships of the team with players. During these meetings, the team can criticise individual behaviours which appear to be unnecessarily aggressive;
- replace systematically any team member when it is realised they are worn out by the relationship.

3. *Systematise the relationship.* The change which is under way will not happen in one event. It will happen by successive discoveries in the same way that one buys a new house. The help relationship establishes itself with time and this is the problem: the project team is so busy that once someone has been convinced, their support is taken as permanent and one moves to the next player. However, if the allies do not feel supported in their actions, they will quickly give up.

To achieve this, regular meetings to keep in touch should be set up with allies to help manage the relationship. These will provide opportunities to maintain their determination to support the project. A simple presentation, and even three months of training, will not guarantee that the players will do what is expected of them, even if they have committed themselves. One must regularly rekindle their desires, just as the Olympic flame is rekindled every four years, and inspire them with the right ideas to get them to move to the next step. So, first and foremost the project manager must be an organiser of meetings and of individual follow-ups which allow the group of allies to progress towards the objective.

4. *Clarify and openly express what the allies only perceive vaguely and embark upon with hesitation.* For many people, help consists of saying what must be done. Rogers has a different view. He recommends that one should not say what has to be done, but describe the situation in clear terms for the other party who will then be in a position to find a solution. The aim is not just to get someone to understand by a succession of clever questions. The objective is more to give words and images to allies so that they can make up their minds and act. In order to achieve this, the authors as consultants, bring in what is called methodological support.

PAVING THE WAY FOR ACTION WITH METHODOLOGICAL SUPPORT

Quite often allies are neither professionals of change nor people used to tense situations. A mediation–revelation process might have strongly motivated them to support the project, but this motivation is not enough. They won't know what to do, or they might undertake useless or dangerous actions. One must first listen to them and be in a position to allow them to understand and to act effectively.

Of course the first method one needs to share with the allies is the lateral project, as described in the first three parts of this book. It must become *the* common language of all the allies.

But the demands which must be responded to are often more specific and concrete:

1. People have great difficulty in *analysing the sociodynamics of the players* around them. They ask for help.
2. People have considerable difficulty in discussing together the implementation strategies to adopt. Even when they agree on the objective, everyone holds their ground. They ask for help to reach an agreement.
3. People have *considerable difficulty in planning their time* and in breaking actions into steps. They ask for help to plan their actions.
4. People find it difficult to get *a concrete view of the future*. Employees ask for job functions and directors spend their time drawing organisation charts. They ask for help to visualise the future.

HELPING TO IDENTIFY ALLIES

Sociodynamics and segmenting the field of play brings into view for the players a new dimension; this makes it possible to explain phenomena which otherwise would have remained hidden. These are tools to share with first-circle allies. But it is very difficult for people to free themselves from the classical view of the players. Experience has shown that a person is likely to continue with the two analyses simultaneously – the old and the new – without links. They must then be helped to see the field of players in the new way. Their behaviour will be profoundly changed as a result.

150   *Developing the Dynamics of the Lateral Project*

That is why sociodynamics must be presented in ways which take into account the culture of the people involved. The Customer Service Case shows an adaptation of a sociodynamics diagram to a particular situation.

The Surprises of the Motivation/Skills Diagram:
The Customer Service Case

A reorganisation in a large firm has led to a proposal to reduce the size of the customer service department from 70 people to 13 – in other words the loss of 57 jobs. In order to select those who are to lose their jobs, management decides to examine the skills of the 70 employees and categorise them using an evaluation grid which takes into account:

- their capacity to understand customer requirements,
- their knowledge of the procedures for treating requests, and
- the quality of customer service contact.

Staff are then classified into good, average and bad exclusively on the basis of the skills criteria needed to meet the future needs of the organisation. (see Figure 14.1). Two of the strongest opponents to change fall into the *good* category according to the management's selection process.

Let's look at the players from a new angle (see Figure 14.2). This is a grid which allows the evaluation not only of the skills level but also the *level of motivation* of the person. This is the motivation/skills diagram, which values each dimension equally. Looking at the first diagram, which only takes skills into account, opponents are selected to participate in the future service. According to the motivation/skills diagram, it becomes clear that another selection is preferable.

Evaluation

By simply changing the reference diagram, behaviours have been changed, without giving any orders. The method was sufficient.

Helping Allies to Act

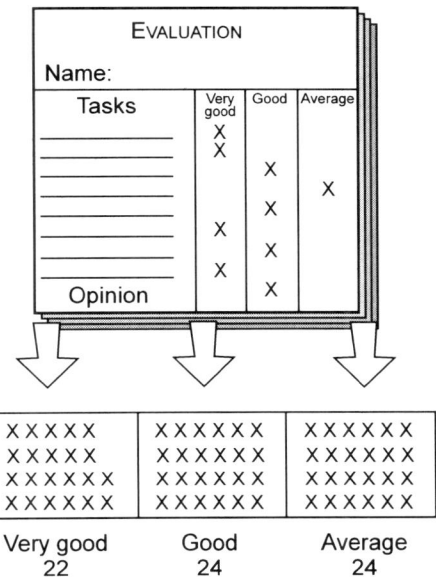

Figure 14.1 Appraisal of staff according to their skills

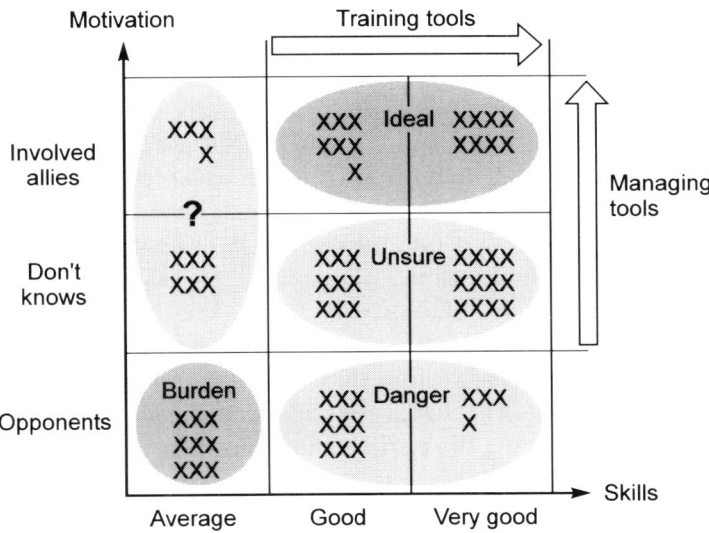

Figure 14.2 Appraisal of staff using the motivation/skills diagram

Let's note an important point about this diagram. Skilled opponents are more dangerous in that they carry the values of skills. They are, in fact, much more dangerous than unskilled opponents whose departure would be less painful.

HELPING TO REACH AGREEMENT

The allies will have to mobilise their teams. They will have to accomplish by themselves what the project managers have already achieved with them, the creation of a circle – this time the second one. Quite often the management does not know how to do this. How can a group of people with differing opinions be made to see eye to eye on sensitive issues without having the team explode?

The scenario method is used to evaluate the consequences of a choice: is it better to construct a motorway or to improve the existing roads in a densely populated area? The method does not look for *the* solution to the problem, but explores the possible scenarios which might provide a solution. One can multiply scenarios, but what is important is that they are defined on a common grid so that they can be compared (see Figures 14.3 and 14.4).

By not presenting *the* solution to a problem, but possible solutions, or by considering solutions not previously thought of, the path is smoothed. This allows individuals to find reasons which justify their support for one particular solution. It is said that the tiger cannot see the prey if the latter remains still. It cannot distinguish it from the background as long as the prey does not move. In the same way, people have trouble perceiving change if they cannot put it into perspective with an alternative.

The scenario method enables individuals to react when a simple presentation of a unique solution would have left them speechless. The participants criticise the chosen scenario. They propose others. They start to get into the subject, and to find solutions that no one had thought of. This allows one to specify the real consequences of each scenario on each participant, so improving the participants' knowledge of the subject.

The scenario method also has the advantage of giving names to options, which makes it much easier for participants to differentiate between them. There may be the 'Churchill' scenario against the 'Garibaldi' scenario. Instead of arguing over detail it is the strategic options which are tackled and discussed. This apparently quite simple tool enables allies who do not know how to approach their teams to discover a constructive dynamic with them.

The names of the scenarios must not involve moral judgements →

	Scenario 1	Scenario 2	Scenario 3
Name	Classic	Specialised	Adapted
Main topic	Focused on professional branches	Focused on the meeting points	Focused on foreign sectors
Organisation chart	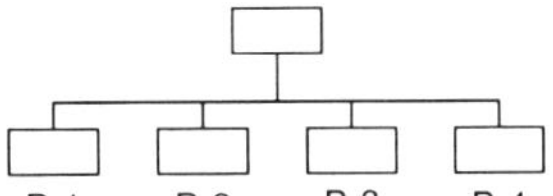 Directors / Asst. Directors / Br1 Br2 Br3 Br4	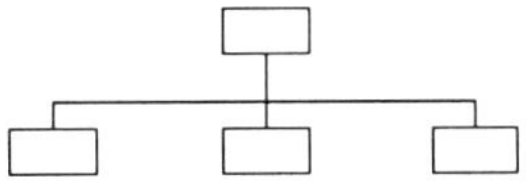 Directors / Asst. Directors / Regional Control Training	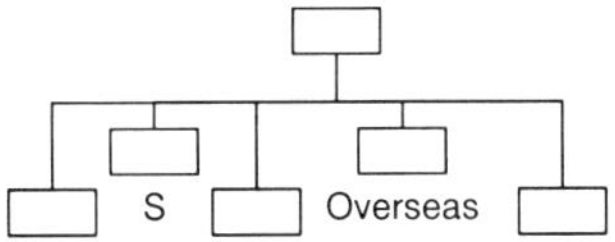 Directors / Asst. Directors / N S E Overseas Commonwealth
Number of workers required	28	32	42
Number of middle managers	4	3	5
Number of head clerks	12	12	15

← The analysis grid is independent of the scenario

Figure 14.3 An example of how scenarios are described

153

Evaluation criteria	Notes		
	Scenario 1	Scenario 2	Scenario 3
Name	Classic	Specialised	Adapted
Visibility from the outside	1 1 1 3 1 1 1 1 1 2 1 (1.4)	3 3 3 1 3 3 3 3 3 3 (2.8)	2 2 2 1 2 2 2 2 2 3 (2)
Acceptability to the staff	3 3 1 3 2 1 3 2 1 2 (2.1)	2 2 2 2 2 2 1 2 2 2 (1.9)	1 3 1 1 1 1 3 1 1 2 (1.5)
Technical practicality	3 3 1 3 3 3 2 3 3 3 (2.6)	2 2 1 2 1 2 2 1 1 1 (1.5)	1 1 1 1 1 1 2 1 1 2 (1.2)
Budgetary feasibility	2 2 2 1 2 1 2 1 3 1 (1.7)	2 3 1 3 3 3 1 3 3 3 (2.5)	1 1 1 1 1 1 1 1 1 1 (1)
Acceptability to the company	2 2 1 2 1 2 2 1 1 1 (1.5)	3 3 1 3 2 1 1 3 2 1 (2)	1 1 3 3 1 1 1 1 1 1 (1.4)
Opinions	1 1 1 1 1 1 1 1 1 1 (1)	2 2 2 3 1 2 2 2 2 2 (2)	3 3 3 1 3 3 3 3 2 3 (2.7)

Figure 14.4 Evaluation of scenarios by the management team

HELPING TO PLAN ACTIONS

For players who are unaccustomed to change, the greatest difficulty is to plan their actions. For many players life is quite normal: key decisions are made for them. To embark on a project and assume responsibility for it assumes that one has an understanding of the management of classical projects and, therefore, planning. For most players this is not so. The most frequently asked questions are: how do I plan? where do I start? what do I do next?

Retro-planning, as its name suggests, sounds a rather backward method of planning, but it is very useful. It lists all the tasks which must be completed to achieve the objective, and works backwards to find the

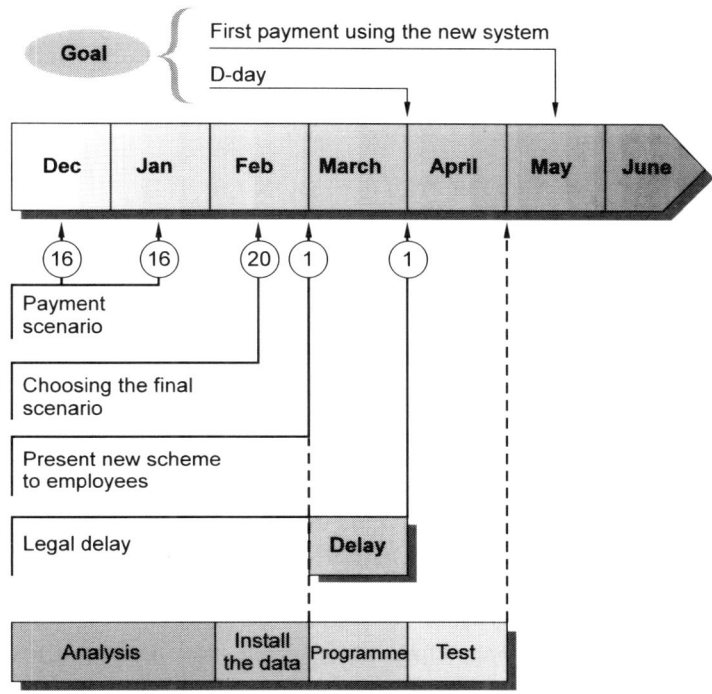

Figure 14.5 Retro-planning for a project to change the way employees are paid

tasks which need be tackled first (see Figure 14.5). This tool is extremely useful in encouraging a player to take action because:

- It *sets a concrete objective*. For retro-planning one must have a finish date: one must be able to say: 'On Monday 10 May, we must move into the new building'.
- It *lets the players understand the objective*. Many people give their agreement on impulse, but fail to evaluate the amount of work which their commitment will mean.
- It allows one to *say very definitely what needs to be done tomorrow morning*.

It is this last aspect which is most interesting. Those with no experience of managing projects find it difficult to find a definite link between an objective – which may be three months, six months or a year away – with actions which need to be carried out tomorrow. A game of questions and answers can help a player to define a process which, in turn leads him or her to act.

HELPING FORM A CONCRETE VISION OF THE FUTURE

In most sensitive projects the discussions, the criticisms and the tensions are all essentially caused by the fact that unbiased facts are missing which can help people judge a future situation or the consequences of a choice.

Great management ideas flourish: the customer is king; total quality control; training for everyone; productivity must increase, and so on. But, realistically, what most people are asking is: what are the consequences of this change on their jobs, workloads and their environment. Worse, often no one has taken the time to examine the day-to-day implications of the change, and the fear of the unknown is the main barrier to change. This is why the authors have developed a tool which forces those who propose change and those who will implement it, *to forecast the consequences of the change on the daily tasks of the people concerned.*

This tool is the chrono-structure and it comes from a simple idea. Every change is going to have a consequence on the *time* one spends on one's tasks. In order to master change, one must first evaluate its impact on the chrono-structure: in other words, on the organisation of the time of the people concerned.

This tool has two added features: the chrono-budget which is very general, and the chrono-planner which is extremely detailed. The chrono-budget of a person is the way that person allocates his or her time in a year, a month or a week. There would be, for example, a chrono-budget before the change and a chrono-budget after the change. The chrono-planner is the implementation of a chrono-budget of a person on a day-by-day basis. For example, one would undertake a chrono-planner for a typical week, a typical month, a typical year.

There is, of course, no point in imposing a chrono-budget and a chrono-planner on a person. The objective is to ask people to do their own chrono-budget and chrono-planner, starting from what they understood of the proposed change. The results are discussed in a group with the rest of the team, and the group then considers the implications of the changes. Of course, it is this discussion and this follow-up which allows everyone to understand the change and to adapt it to the real situation on the ground.

The Use of a Chrono-Budget: The Social Service Case

The management of a regional social service institution wants to develop a partnership so that its employees can work with other organisations. The institution's role is to provide residential care (accommodation, education, training, clothing, sports, etc.) for young people who have been convicted of a crime but find themselves in high-risk family situations. Its bigger mission is to find a way to reintroduce these young people into society so that they can become useful citizens. The problem is that the institution operates on only a very brief part of the young person's life.

Youngsters cannot regain social norms without taking into account what they have experienced before and what they are going to experience after their time in the institution. (Over half are repeat offenders.) In order to be successful in its mission, the institution must develop relationships with other organisations which take care of the young, including:

- the secondary school, and the professional training services of the state;
- the teachers of the home area where the crimes were committed; and
- the police from the home area.

An important national reform – the Partnership Project – has already started in this direction. The legislation to impose this Partnership Project fundamentally changes the way the institution is organised. In fact, no one really understands what must be changed. Staff believe that the Partnership Project is either something which is already being done or something extra to their normal work.

The objective is to make the Partnership Project understood and to see how it can be developed. With the management team, a chrono-budget is launched which consists of (see Figure 14.6):

- Listing the activities of the institution, identifying who operates them and how much time they take. Preparing the chrono-budget is undertaken jointly with the consultants.
- Activity by activity, defining how each activity is related to the Partnership Project and to what extent.
- Seeing how much time one must give to these new tasks and how the chrono-budget must be reorganised.

158 *Developing the Dynamics of the Lateral Project*

Tasks	N.G.	C.L.	C.B.	M.K.	J.P.P.	M.Z.	F.R.
Working agreements	15	15	12	12	12	12	12
Managing meetings for regional management	3	40		5	4	1	
Managing DSQ–CCPD devices	1	20	10	2	2	2	2
Conceiving and implementing a communications policy	4			4	16	4	
Conceiving and implementing a mechanism for a better understanding of the law	55	30	30	30	30	30	20
Managing a concentration device	5			8	1		
Establishing new relations with the media	3		24				24
Managing the regional accommodation policy				12			5
Managing a policy of cultural and artistic expression		15					
Managing the regional computer system	10	3	8	8	12	8	40
Managing staff training	2			12	12	2	12
Managing a sports policy	4	2	4			120	
Total of worked days on contract	195	212	199	145	208	255	213
Number of days theoretically planned on contract	179	194	199	199	199	199	199
Difference	–16	–18	0	54	–9	–56	–14

Team members (N.G., C.L., C.B., M.K., J.P.P., M.Z., F.R.)

Figure 14.6 Example of a chrono-budget

Evaluation

By speaking specifically of the time of each action, the reality of the reform has taken shape, first for the management and then for the staff. They have been able very specifically to construct their own contributions to the politics of the Partnership.

This discussion enabled them, starting with a common language – time (in this particular case, days) – to quantify each task and understand its content.

For example, the management of the relationship with a government department was scaled back from 10 days a year to 2 days a year. In discussions it was clear that the days saved would be more efficient if they were allocated to finding accommodation in the community for the young offenders.

Thanks to this method, which had operated in a particularly tense atmosphere, the project moved forward, whereas originally every one had agreed to the new partnership without changing anything to the normal functioning of the service. The chrono-budget made it possible to think in months. The chrono-planner allows one to get specifically into the future organisation in which people will find themselves and to get things done.

The Use of the Chrono-Planner: The Union School Case

A trade union decides to create a school for its members. Its main aims are the development of regional training leaders whose job consists of:

- identifying needs (who are the new union representatives to be trained?);
- organising the training sessions;
- leading the training sessions; and
- communicating with union members to sell training.

Using the allies' strategy a dozen volunteers are selected. Following a mediation–revelation exercise this team declares itself to be interested, but they have one over-riding fear: are they good enough for the job?

On analysis, it is evident that the team has not got the first idea on the practical organisation of such a post. They are trade unionists: they are not trainers much less managers. Their questions are: what does it mean, very specifically, 'to identify the training needs' or 'to organise a training session' or 'to communicate with the workers?' The source of concern is not so much the skills that need to be acquired but the central question: 'What shall we do and how shall we organise ourselves?'

The authors worked with them to develop a chrono-budget for their jobs. This gave, first, a comprehensive list of the tasks to be done and, second, the time to dedicate to each task.

But this was still too vague for them. How are all these tasks interlinked? There then followed, step by step, the chrono-planning of the job (see Figure 14.7). Working together with the authors, the links between these tasks were defined – hour by hour, day by day showing them what they are going to do with 220 days of work.

160 *Developing the Dynamics of the Lateral Project*

Sample week					
Time	Day 1	Day 2	Day 3	Day 4	Day 5
08.00–09.30		Recruitment	Recruitment	Recruitment	Recruitment
09.30–12.30		Interviews	Interviews	Interviews	Writing reports
12.30–14.00					
14.00–16.30	Personal follow up	Personal follow up	Outside meeting	Personal follow up	Weekly evaluation summary
16.30–18.00			Introduction to the unions		

Figure 14.7 Chrono-planning post training

In this way there was agreement on what they would do Monday morning at 9.00 a.m. and the third Tuesday of the month at 3.00 p.m. The key point is to get the plan discussed, and their motivation increased as they understood how they were going to achieve their roles.

Evaluation

Although they had never been trainers, or responsible for training, the team put 400 trade unionists through courses in their first year and established the concept of a school organisation.

The chrono-planner system might be linked to the sophrology of organisations. The greatest sportsmen and women use sophrology, that is auto-suggestion; they place less emphasis on physical exercises and instead develop mental training. They prepare in their mind, with the help of a trainer, for the grand final. Through thought they rewind the film of a future game: starting in the changing room and forecasting every instant, every incident, every noise. On the day of the final, they are ready.

POINTS TO REMEMBER

- It is the action of the allies which really makes projects happen. It is important to help them in this task to prevent them from:
  - stopping at the first difficulty encountered; or
  - following a path other than the one agreed on.
- To help one's allies is not a simple operation, especially in stressful situations. To motivate them to act without taking action oneself one must respect four principles:
  - intervene only when asked;
  - adopt an open attitude (empathy, positive feelings, authenticity);
  - create a close relationship to implement systems to manage the relationship; and
  - offer them methods to understand and act (sociodynamics, segmenting the field of play, retro-planning, scenario methods, chrono-structure).

15 Adapting a Project in Real Time According to Events and Micro-Events

The strategy of the lateral project is not about modifying the project to meet some hypothetical demand as a one-off initiative, and then managing it as if all the problems had been solved. On the contrary, the project is managed by putting the energy of the players first and technique second – and doing this for the total lifetime of the project. Each day brings new actions and new events to react to, and one must then 'lateralise the lateral project'. The project must be adapted in real time taking into account current conditions on the ground.

The energy that players are ready to dedicate to a project depends on their opinions of it. Yet, in more than 100 projects in which the authors have been involved, there has been one constant: there is an incredible gap between what managers want to do and the perceptions people have of their intentions.

A COMMON LANGUAGE: THE SIGNIFICANT FACTS OR MICRO-EVENTS

Whilst one's eyes admire the panoramic view of the mountains after four hours walking, the feet only feel the interior of the shoe and curse whoever put them in. For the majority of players, the project is not the well-constructed and homogenous entity as it is viewed by the management. *Their point of view is very different*: it comes from what they have learnt and what they feel at a particular moment. The project is probably going to be 'an event' for the players. More precisely, a certain number of significant facts or 'micro-events' are going to make the event: the announcement of the nomination of the project leader, a press release from government, the launching of a report, the arrival of boxes left casually in a corridor.

These micro-events are self-explanatory one thinks. Not at all! The interpretation which the players will put on these events depends totally on their own environment which can be far removed from that of the project leaders. For example, people may know that the project leader was previously involved in a redundancy programme in which 200 people lost their jobs and now his nickname is the 'axe-man'. From this they infer that redundancies are imminent.

So project managers are advised to take an interest in these micro-events which are a concrete manifestation of the project for the players. It is by mastering the meaning that the players place on these micro-events that one will be able to win them over. If need be, one must take measures to ensure that the desired meaning is conveyed and not that of opponents.

In order to succeed in a sensitive project, one must adapt it and lateralise it, one micro-event at a time. This is the object of the political and social 'watch' envisioned by Jean-Christian Fauvet in the late 1970s, which the authors have developed and called 'event-management'. First, let's examine those micro-events which are of interest to the project.

An micro-event is a fact which is relevant to a player. For example, a computer breakdown is a significant fact for secretaries concerning the poor quality of the IT system. It leads them to be very cautious about a project that involves IT. It is a fact. It has meaning. If one wants to introduce a new computer system, this fact has meaning for the project leaders.

In a sensitive project, the definition of an event is not the common one. Usually an event is an *exceptional* fact and concerns *everyone*, but in a sensitive project an event or micro-event is in fact of *limited scope* which may only be of concern to *some players. An event is also a date.* A fact has no date, but an event is dated. It is the moment when a player learns about a fact. For example, the day that one hears that there is to be a new photocopying machine; then the day that one notes that it has not arrived; then the day when it is delivered which does not correspond with the original date.

Facts are only interesting to the extent that they are a novelty for those who perceive them. For example, the tenth issue of a company newsletter is not a novelty if everyone knows that, having read the nine preceding ones, there is nothing interesting in it. In the same way once the photocopying machine is installed, it is no longer an event. The most important moment for the project is the moment a player learns a fact. That is the moment one needs to be there.

Let's examine the feelings of a secretary who is working in a bank about to install a new computer system. The training programme has been announced to staff, and 15 days beforehand four boxes of equipment arrive and are left untidily in a corridor. No one knows anything, but this is not unusual. The computer specialists have mastered the art of delivering equipment days before installation, leaving their boxes to litter corridors and causing total chaos.

A week before training, a technician comes to unpack the boxes and accidentally shuts down the computer system while trying to install a plug. Three days before the training the secretary in the training department rings to check that the room is ready. It isn't. Solutions are sought, etc., etc. Often, this is how people on the ground feel about sensitive projects. Beginning with this type of malfunctioning, tension rises, little by little.

There is no need to be aware of each and every one of the micro-events just described to know that there is a problem. One is enough to prompt emergency measures. This is why the level of accuracy concerning the dates of micro-events is not the real problem – they might be grossly inaccurate – what matters is that one really starts from the anxieties of the players.

An micro-event must concern the project. The link, however, may be tenuous. For example, the arrival of the photocopying machine might be relevant to the project because it shows that the working conditions of employees are taken into account.

One can deliberately choose to give meaning to some micro-events that are apparently not linked to the project. For example, a retirement party could be organised for an employee who has spent 50 years with the company. He or she might say: 'I am sad to be leaving so soon as I will be missing a great experience'. Often, this is how the meaning of the project can be enriched in terms of desires and values.

But others can also give meaning to a fact which may seem insignificant in the precise context of the project. For example, the explosion at Chernobyl nuclear power station can be used against a company manufacturing radio-isotopes for medicinal purposes.

There are four types of event or micro-event which are of interest in sensitive projects:

1. Events and micro-events *which are directly associated with the project* and which can *be predicted from the start*. For example, for a project to investigate a site for the disposal of radioactive wastes, it might be the arrival of the first trucks at the site. These events are the simplest to manage because one has time to plan appropriate communications. However, just because events are predictable does not always mean that they are predicted.

2. Events and micro-events *which are directly associated with the project* but which *cannot be predicted*. For example, a truck accidentally kills a worker. These events are the most difficult to manage. First, they are generally very negative with regard to the project and, second, because one must work with some urgency, mistakes can be made.
3. *Predictable* events and micro-events which *are not directly associated with the project*, but which can have a strong influence on how the project is interpreted by the players. For example, a competitor announces an increase in market share.
4. Events and micro-events which *are not directly linked to the project* and which *cannot be predicted*. For example, a customer cancels an order because of a late delivery, but the project will mean shorter delivery times.

KNOWING OF EVENTS AND MICRO-EVENTS PREFERABLY IN ADVANCE

How can one know of events in advance? This is the main problem; one does not know of events and micro-events as they are seen by the players. One knows of one's own events, for example:

- the date of a switch to the new IT system;
- the official opening of the factory by a local dignitary; or
- the signing of a major contract with government officials.

There is a simple way to find out about the players' events and micro-events: simply ask them.

In Part I, segmenting the field of play allowed the creation of imaginary sectors on a human scale. In each sector, one or more allies who can provide information are identified. When it is noticed that there is no ally in a sector, everything possible is done to put one there. So the field of play is covered with a network of identified allies: an information *collection network*. These allies can be management, trainers, union representatives, councillors or journalists.

A system for collecting information must be in place. In fact allies will not pass events or micro-events to the project team if they are not asked to, or, rather they will not do so systematically. They may pass on a negative event occasionally to alert the project team that they are not on top of things, but they will not do a systematic and homogenous job. A good collection network revolves around four principles:

Adapting a Project in Real Time 167

- a cycle;
- a responsible person;
- a method; and
- support for the collection, a database classified by date.

First, there is the need for a *cycle*. Knowing about events or micro-events cannot be achieved – for the whole lifetime of a project – by a one-off interview with allies. There is a need for regular information throughout. Likewise there is little point in asking: 'Pass me on information about events when you find out about them', as there is the risk that the information will be late or partial. There is thus a need to fix a cycle to collect information. In a crisis this could be daily or weekly. In normal times it could be monthly, or quarterly for more remote players. The rhythm has another advantage: little by little, events become clearer. Something which was missed first time round is picked up the next time, so the quality of the information improves.

Someone must be *responsible*. He or she *must come from a third party* because otherwise the facts that are fed back might be biased. The person responsible for the collection network has the exclusive mission of being on the ground and regularly informed. The importance of third parties has already been emphasised in Part III of this book.

There is also a need for a *method*. The collation of a list of events and micro-events uses an interview technique that needs some special skills. Interviewees know of the events and micro-events that are going to affect them, but they might not be conscious of them. They don't think in terms of events. Therefore, it is not sufficient to ask the simple question: 'What is going to happen?' The technique used is similar to that used in qualitative market research.

Finally there is a need to *support the collection* of information. If this work is seriously carried out one will have an important list of events and micro-events. It is quite common to have 250 events 'on the books'. These might be relatively old or, on the contrary, they might relate to next year.

A computer database is the ideal way to list events and micro-events, as it is easy to manipulate. Events are listed in date order and are regularly updated. Such a list of micro-events (see Figure 15.1) becomes a form of alternative planning. The company's plan is *its vision* of the project whereas the list of events and micro-events is the project *as seen by the players*. This simple knowledge, in itself, gives good feedback. One knows the list is of good quality when managers learn something by reading it. For example, they learn that there was a meeting of the sales force last week when they were supposed to be in the field. Or they will learn that

LIST OF EVENTS

Date	Field of play	Events	Decision date			
1/11	2	Return from Moscow of the technical team	5/10		X	X
2/11	3	Opening of the new South Building	5/10	X	X	
7/11	1	First meeting of the quality-control team	15/10		X	
15/11	3	Presentation of the audit report on the research department	8/7	X	X	
18/11	1	Mailing of greeting card to the staff	8/7		X	X
28/11	2	Welcome reception for foreign research workers	5/10			X
1/12	4	Implementation of the new computer program	15/10	X		
3/12	2	Meeting of the joint production committee about 'Downsizing program'	8/7		X	
4/12	1	Launching of the new purchasing campaign	15/10		X	X
5/12	4	End-of-year bonus	8/8	X		

- Field of play from which the information is received
- Date of event
- Events card / Description / To do
- Date of decision
- To know which part of the strategy is highlighted

Figure 15.1 List of events

the switch to a new IT system in one office is running two months late. But listing events only allows the project management to react to events, it is not yet ready for action: this is the real management of events.

TO MANAGE AN EVENT IS TO ADAPT IT OR TO ADAPT THE PROJECT

Some years ago a few days after a massive storm an advertisement appeared for a car, noted for its robustness, on which a large tree had fallen. There was a simple picture caption: 'The owner of this car got out alive and once the tree was taken away, he drove home without incident. The bodywork needed some attention.'

Readers of the newspaper were reminded of the storm and of the dozens of cars which were wrecked. With a few words, and without adding any extra facts, the manufacturer had added another glorious chapter to the car's legendary reputation for robustness. By playing on the storm, a much greater impact had been produced compared to any other style of advertising. It is worth noting that anyone who saw the actual car could have formed a reverse interpretation to that given by the advertisement. What is the point of putting so much money in a car when it can be crushed by a tree?

The objective of event management is to keep the project alive within each micro-event, by taking account of the situation (see Figure 15.2). The challenge is to bridge the gap between the event and what one is trying to say, and this articulation is not always easy to find. Say a firm announces

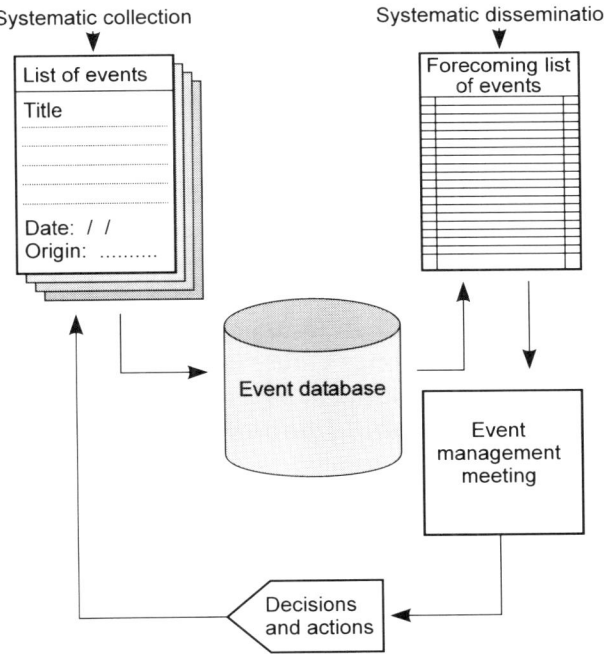

Figure 15.2 Management of micro-events

the launch of an IT project which should increase sales and so preserve jobs and, at the same time, announces plans for 250 redundancies. Naturally, employees will link both events and will assume they are being lied to. It is not easy to explain that the two events are not linked, and the most usual reaction 'not to realise' that there is a contradiction is the avoidance syndrome outlined in Part I.

Determination on the part of management is needed to find a dialogue to explain the contradiction; for example, by showing that those made redundant do not have the right qualifications to be involved in the IT project. This is, of course, easier if the opposite was not said when the project was launched.

Quite often the articulation in terms of usefulness – that is rational arguments – is quite simple to find. What is more difficult, however, is to ensure the proper perception in terms of the desires and values of the people concerned. For example, take an event such as the installation of a new computer system. A meeting is planned with coffee and biscuits with a high-powered presentation by the head of the IT project. But, it might well be that the presentation might totally terrorise a secretary (negative desire) and get on the nerves of the head of the department (negative value) because he or she was not consulted in advance. It is far more difficult to bring values and desires to life for each event and micro-event. Therefore this is where effort must be concentrated.

The mediation–revelation process should have identified the shortcomings in the project as regards the players' needs in terms of desires and values. The lateral project, which normally responds to these needs, must be the reference for devising messages suited to these targets.

To manage an event is to envisage a scenario that allows the modification of the original plan. For example, in the case of the computerisation of the accident department of an insurance company, the scenario was modified to start with the director's office rather than those of the writers. This decision went against the initial plan and met with opposition from the head of the computer project. However, it was worthwhile because as a result the system was well accepted by the rest of the staff.

But managing events and micro-events means that at the next collection of events it may turn out that a scenario was a failure. The allies on the ground will inform the project management that the players have reacted badly. One must adapt immediately and try a more suitable scenario. Communication of a project is not independent from a project, it is an integral part of it. To master this communication one must descend to the level of detail of both the scenario and the form of communication. To change the form, one must adapt the content.

MAKING DIRECT CONTACT SYSTEMATICALLY WITH THE PLAYERS

Players form opinions on a project, progressively, by adding successive events and micro-events that are sometimes contradictory. People get to know about events in a variety of ways including reading about them, informal conversations with a friend, or during training or at a meeting. In fact, a player is likely to hear different versions of the same event. And each time a new or complementary interpretation will add to the proceeding ones.

These micro-events and the meanings that the players give to them are transmitted to other players through *communication channels*. A channel of communication is the means by which one can make contact with a player. Conversations between neighbours is a channel; as is the reading of a newspaper or a brochure, or attending a training seminar.

In fact, the key question is not just: 'How do players know about events and micro-events?', but 'How can we transmit our interpretation of events to them?' 'What communication channels can be used or which ones can be created?' It is obvious that the project's management cannot be involved in all informal conversations such as those at dinner parties or over the garden fence. However, there are a few communications channels where the project can have a presence in an enduring and systematic way. There are four types: (see Figure 15.3):

- *Media channels* such as brochures, newspapers, advertising, television or radio. Press releases, direct mail, brochure distribution and posters also fall into this category as do company announcements on notice boards.
- The *group channel*, for example a management meeting, a Tupperware party, an exhibition or a training session. These channels are distinguished from interpersonal channels (the next category) as they generate a *group effect*, the importance of which has already been noted. So user-groups or conferences with elected representatives can be organised; or a management meeting can 'toast' the arrival and commissioning of a new piece of equipment.
- *Interpersonal channels* are the one-to-one, face-to-face relationships. As described in the section on 'doing the rounds', mediation–revelation is an interpersonal channel, as is door-to-door selling.
- *Factual channels* are those which lead to formation of a direct opinion of an event. The Apostle, St ('Doubting') Thomas said: 'I do not believe what I do not see', so he was a follower of factual channels. Several players are like St Thomas. A visit to a factory, training at a test site, the borrowing of equipment are all factual channels.

		Feedback capacity	Reaction capacity
Media channels	Press relations Booklets Posters	→ Weak → None → None	→ Weak → None → None
Group channels	Induction meeting Staff committee	→ Good → Good	→ Average → Average
Interpersonal channels	Individual meeting Doing the rounds Collecting the events	→ Excellent → Excellent → Excellent	→ Good → Good → Good
Factual channels	Training at a site Visit to a pilot site Exhibition	→ Good → Good → Good	→ Excellent → Excellent → Excellent

Figure 15.3 The four types of communication channels and their main features

Assuming these categories, it is obvious that generally we do not use that many. Additionally, the coverage of our target audiences – the number of people reached by the communications channels used – is very small; so the target audience is not getting the messages. The channels form a communication system for each individual player. Experience shows that each person has their favourite channel of communication. One manager may prefer media channels (using notice boards), another the group channel (off-the-record briefings with journalists), and another will try interpersonal channels (by being on the shop floor with a word for everyone).

This distinction between the different channels of communication is important as most managers prefer media channels over others. However, *these are not suitable for sensitive projects because they do not allow quick feedback*. Media channels are preferred because they are the easiest to use: they allow the rapid production of a statement which can be transmitted to a large number of people almost instantaneously. A government communications adviser told his minister: 'We must be able to respond while the issue is still live'. He first published a newspaper which was printed overnight and distributed door-to-door the next day. In so doing, he was trying to impose the same message on everyone but this would be ridiculed by many of the players as the arguments were too general. He was also bypassing his allies by putting himself in the line of fire. It was a good Samurai strategy suited to Type-1 projects, not a players' strategy adapted to a sensitive project.

In addition, media channels are not very expensive per contact. The cost of an advertisement in a newspaper or a direct mail shot is a few pennies for each person reached. A note on a notice board requires 15 minutes to write and a few pence to photocopy. Of course media channels are, in principle, intellectually pleasing: they are generally quite elegant, they allow a consistent and well thought-out argument which can be read and corrected before dissemination and, more importantly, one can delegate production to an advertising agency, which means they take little time to manage.

By contrast, *non-media channels are expensive and difficult to use*. If one has forgotten to say something during a meeting, one cannot get all the participants together again for some time. They are also very slow channels. One cannot assemble people today for a meeting tomorrow; a room has to be found and people persuaded to turn up. In addition, they are very expensive channels. Organisational expenses such as the salary costs of the project staff, the travel expenses, room hire – everything costs thousands of times more than a sheet of paper on a notice board.

It can seem like an insurmountable hurdle if one has to organise partners' meetings, client meetings and employee meetings. Interpersonal contact would seem to be a non-runner if there are 100 people to see: each meeting will take up to an hour which amounts to almost 15 man-days (the cost of a visit by a sales representative is estimated at £100 per visit). However, despite their seemingly overwhelming advantages over other channels, the media channels have two characteristics which make them unsuitable:

1. They have a very weak capacity for feedback. Between the despatching of a letter and the moment first reactions are known, a minimum of a week will have passed and as the former British Prime Minister Harold Wilson said: 'A week is a long time in politics.'
2. They have a tendency to solidify positions and to simplify messages. By their very nature, media channels prefer strong messages with big headlines which can attract attention. An environmentalist dressed as a skeleton and carrying a drum with Radioactive Waste on it and a nuclear holocaust poster, is more sensational (especially for the media) than the well-thought-out arguments of a scientist who is discussing the pros and cons of the project.

On the other hand, the interpersonal and group channels have a very interesting characteristic. One is face to face with the person, and so can get an immediate and direct reaction and adapt an argument to the reaction received. This capacity to adapt to local realities is one of the fundamental points in the management of a sensitive project.

To take an example that is highly relevant: one never knows if a note on a notice board is read or not. On the other hand, one knows immediately

- if someone has come to a meeting;
- if the person has day-dreamed or asked questions; or
- if someone displayed antagonism or synergy.

Therefore the question to ask is not: 'shall I make contact or not', but 'how can I be in direct contact more often with my targets?'

DEVELOPING NON-MEDIA CHANNELS

One of the reasons often quoted for not using interpersonal channels is that 'it cannot be managed'. One hears, 'Oh, that's impossible to organise'. Not only is it possible to organise interpersonal contact, but it is vital in order to manage a tense situation. What is a sales network if not the organisation of interpersonal channels with customers? The idea is to organise contact with players with the same diligence that is applied to one's sales network.

Two types of organised interpersonal channels have already been described in this book:

- *Segmenting the field of play*, which segments an area into homogenous groups of human size, and designates to each a unique contact and ally; and
- *Doing the rounds* (of meetings), which means organising one-to-one visits on a systematic basis with a selection of people.

The framework which constitutes these two types of interpersonal channels can be applied to many situations.

Segmenting the Field of Play: The Urban Transport Case

A transport company manages a bus network for an average-sized city. It employs 200 bus drivers who work by shift, from five o'clock in the morning till midnight. The bus drivers' job is one with little scope for progression: starting at age 20 until retirement at 55, they generally do exactly the same thing – drive a bus. Once they have seen the 20 bus routes of the network, they have seen everything.

For historical reasons there is no management hierarchy for the drivers – the core responsibilities are spread between the directors:

- One takes care of human resources, for example absenteeism, recruitment, salaries, pensions, etc.
- Another is in charge of planning; on which route and at which time each bus driver is scheduled.
- A third takes care of buying buses, maintenance, new equipment, etc.
- The fourth is responsible for sales and marketing; tickets, prices, advertising, customer relations, etc.
- A fifth focuses on quality of service with the help of inspectors who punch tickets and fine fare dodgers.

So, the 200 bus drivers have no management. For each type of problem there is a different person responsible who is only interested in his or her area of responsibility, not the driver.

The company has an objective to increase profits, but every time a new initiative is launched it is rejected by the bus drivers. The management says that the drivers are refusing to accept change. An analysis shows that, in fact, the initiatives do not take into account the concerns of the drivers, like improving safety in dangerous neighbourhoods or adapting turnaround times to the density of traffic. But this is not surprising – the management see themselves as technicians and their projects are focused on techniques. Not one of them knows what a driver's life is like. In fact, the only people that are ready to listen to the drivers, whether on personal or professional issues, are the union representatives. They are the only people who are capable of giving information on incidents which concern the drivers.

What can be done? Quite simply, the management has to go on to the shop-floor and make contact with the drivers by speaking to them. The field of play must be segmented: each director is assigned to a group of drivers. In the initial stages the objective is to get the directors to know their 'godchildren', to listen to their problems, their suggestions, to be aware of forthcoming events as they are perceived by the drivers.

The first challenge is to prepare the launch of the next annual plan by taking into account grassroots feelings about difficulties, and suggestions from these godchildren. Segmenting the field of play does not just happen. Before the directors become accustomed to it they have to be helped with the smallest of details. This includes detailed prompts for their meetings such is their deeply ingrained fear of contact. They must be convinced that each action can be done without opposition from the unions; the unions serving as an excuse to do nothing.

- First there is a round of mediation–revelation with the directors, to take into account their problems.
- Then, once the team has agreed, a monthly meeting is instituted to manage tensions. This meeting enables each of the directors to review what has been done and to uncover difficulties which have been encountered and to propose solutions.

Evaluation

Within three months there is a considerable improvement in the climate:

- the detailed sociodynamic maps of the drivers for each project are known;
- the directors adapt the project, by themselves, according to suggestions they have received on the ground; and
- they become conscious of the fact that they are not treating the employees' problems at all, and that much more could be achieved with a little money.

The Meeting Round: The Centralisation of Purchasing Case

A large distribution group has introduced a new central buying strategy that is difficult to implement, as it represents in effect, a revolution in the company's culture. Previously the department heads had control of purchasing for their branch. It was, it must be admitted, the fun part of their jobs, whereas with the new strategy they feel they have become shelf-stackers. Obviously, the resistance within the company is stronger than the concept. A round of meetings was organised for the company's managing director with the department heads – about 100 people. In order to do this, two strategies were used:

- An analysis of the chrono-structure of the director, that is the way he allocated his time to the tasks in hand. He was shown that he could delegate some tasks and free himself two days a week to

organise the round of meetings at the branches. The argument was simple, 'Your time is your strategy. If you cannot spare 40% of your time on a strategic issue, you cannot retain the strategy'.
- A detailed planner which contained a complete list of the department heads. It was shown to the managing director that, with eight meetings a week, he could meet, face to face, all 100 department heads.

The department heads have never seen anything like this, nor has the company. Each department head is surprised (and pleasantly so) that the director comes to see him once, then twice, then three times. Each time he reminds them of what was said the preceding time and he takes into account the difficulties that were encountered.

Evaluation

The change in purchasing strategy went through despite the resistance:

- on the one hand because the heads of departments supported it in the branches (allies' strategy); and
- on the other hand because this round of meetings allowed the managing director to understand why his arguments were not well received, so he had the means to change them. He has added to his project on central buying, a project to promote the head of the sector towards sales management, and has changed the users' interface of the IT system to adapt it to the constraints of the shops.

IMPLEMENTING ANIMATION SYSTEMS

From among the communication channels that are non-media, there emerges what the authors call 'animation systems'. They enable one to keep in contact with certain players and to get them to act together. Animation systems are first characterised by a *rhythm*. In the case of the rounds of meetings, the rhythm is every quarter: every three months the department head is contacted; every three months a meeting reviews work, uncovers events and checks that each employee has been contacted at least once.

The great difference between an animation system and a simple informal contact, or a presentation meeting, is repetition. It is easy to believe, 'Once I have presented the change, once I have people's commitment, everything will have been done'. But a sensitive project cannot be understood at once. *The relationship must be put in place* through an organisation that systematises the contact with players and which allows the management of events once the objective is attained.

The second characteristic of an animation system that works is *the sharing of a common goal*. From the start, the objective of the relationship must be known and clear. This objective can be to ask for advice on events and micro-events, to review progress, to meet new players or to explain the project.

The third characteristic is the work method, that is *the process accepted by the players to attain the common objective*. An event management system which does not rely on a method accepted by all will, little by little, become eroded and reduced to the level of 'pub talk'.

The fourth characteristic of a good animation system is to have one person identified as responsible. As far as possible this person should not be one of those who manages the project. There is a logic to using one of the allies of the first circle to assume this role, and this is also an opportunity to evaluate his or her commitment. The project management will offer support, but the objective is to have someone in charge of the animation system, or better that he or she manages to mobilise a support team.

A system of individual responses is always preferable to media-type communication that is all encompassing.

POINTS TO REMEMBER

- Always be attentive to those micro-events that mark the daily progress of the project.
- One must exploit them, to endow them with a meaning consistent with the project, or to modify the project if needs be. This is the objective of event management.
- Event management does not exist solely for putting events and micro-events in an attractive format. They should be used to gauge feelings on the ground and to adapt communications accordingly, and so adapt the project.

- In order to know of events and micro-events, there must be systematic information collection from networks which have been constructed on the principles of segmenting the field of play.
- A communication channel is a means to get into contact with a player. There are four types:
  - media channels,
  - group channels,
  - interpersonal channels, and
  - factual channels.
- Managers generally prefer media channels, but these are not suited to sensitive projects because they do not allow quick feedback and the messages are too general and shallow.
- The communication of a sensitive project must use a non-media communication channel.
- The animation systems allow players to be put into a dynamic by offering them the structure that enables them to work together.

16 Ensuring the Management Team's Solidarity

Managing lateral projects calls for a coalition strategy; this has many advantages, but one disadvantage – it is more difficult for a group to make a decision than for an individual.

This difficulty is in addition to the many specific difficulties which typify sensitive projects:

1. *Issues are side-stepped by players when they give information because of insincerity or filters.* Players will say yes to please or in order not to explain themselves, and they will generally say yes to opponents for the same reasons.
2. *The information is biased because words do not carry the same meaning for everyone.* People may not realise at the start the scope of what they have been asked to do. So, someone who agrees something at the planning stage may change his or her mind at the implementation phase once there is a realisation of the true nature of what was agreed to.
3. *Management and their staff are under stress*, particularly in the run-up to a conflict and this influences their judgement. In Part I, some typical examples of sensitive projects going astray were described. No member of the team is immune from this.

To lead the project to a successful conclusion, the decision-making system must be tempered or reinforced. In the army, equipment designed for civilian uses is reinforced in preparation for battle to improve resistance to vibration, heat, humidity and shock. In a sensitive project there are also enough vibrations and shocks to justify such measures. Therefore it is important to anticipate the difficulties in decision-making and to take measures to lessen the consequences. The following four measures can help:

- *strengthen* the project manager, by giving him or her authority to make decisions;

- *reinforce* the database so as to have the right information;
- *reinforce* the production of reference documents on the project to ensure that they do not become a source of tension; and
- *prepare* for conflict in order to avoid it.

STRENGTHENING THE PROJECT MANAGER

Among the management principles that are applicable to all projects, there is a necessity to separate those who define needs from those who propose and realise the solution. The first is traditionally called the project manager. He or she decides and pays. The second is the operator, who does the work. For convenience, these descriptions are retained.

Sensitive projects have a particular feature: no matter the amount of care taken to distribute responsibilities, it is extremely difficult to avoid conflicts at the middle-management level of organisation. It will quickly spread to the level of the project manager, even if the latter is not responsible. So, one must prepare at the highest level for the onslaught.

In normal projects it is the technical aspects that are discussed. The decision-making process is normally concerned with financial risks and the political dimension hardly surfaces. Therefore, quite naturally, it is the operator – the engineer – who takes the lead over the project manager. Difficult subjects are dealt with during project meetings or in works meetings with the engineers, not at the political level. The project manager merely agrees to the decisions made.

By contrast, in sensitive projects it is the political aspects that are overwhelming. Whether one likes it or not the project manager will bear the brunt of potential failure. He or she is in the front line and is the first casualty. The operator might possibly be sacrificed – like an electrical fuse – to protect the project manager in the short term, but a fuse can only be used once; it is a one-shot weapon. When a major project is running twice over budget it is not just the operations director whose head is on the block, the chairman is also in the firing line.

There are four methods of strengthening the project manager.

First Method. Attach a Politically Strong Steering Committee

A steering committee is a group of people whom the project manager entrusts to steer the project. It can either be empowered to take decisions or merely consulted. In a normal project one generally creates a steering committee made up of expert technicians, relevant senior managers and key middle managers. However, in the case of a sensitive project it is essential to constitute a steering committee with the true players, who represent a section of part of the population. So, the steering committee becomes a place for the coalition to make decisions. Of course, this does not simplify the decision-making process, but at least it allows the presence of players who will not just give advice, but who will also carry weight on their home turf.

It soon becomes obvious that to create such a committee is not an easy task. Politicians generally have a nose for this type of responsibility and tend to shun it like the plague. Forming a steering committee boils down to creating a coalition and so is the first step in launching a sensitive project. The mediation–revelation process and the definition of the lateral project often helps to create a good steering committee. Ideally, the first Round Table should be composed of allies that are senior in the organisation, or even from outside the organisation, and means will be sought to involve them in the project.

Second Method. Focus the Steering Committee on Event Management

Steering committees usually focus on the technical progress of projects: Is it on time? Is the budget on target? Will it meet the specifications? In a sensitive project, the members of the steering committee are often politicians. They are not interested in the technicalities and they should not be. They are much more concerned to find out if, politically, things are going well and will they continue to do so. By its composition, the members of the steering committee have a role – not only within the framework of the meeting – but also on their home territories.

So the steering committee must be ahead of events and the project must be in perfect synchronisation with it. In order to do this, the committee must be focused on the management of events. It must confirm the events for the coming months and decide on the way to play these events. Event management is therefore the basic tool for managing the steering committee.

Third Method. Separate the Project Manager from the Operator in a Totally Watertight Way

The separation of the project manager and the operator should be a natural one. Experience shows that nothing is more difficult than to limit someone solely to functional decisions. Quite often the project manager is also responsible for technical matters and encroaches on the operator's area. In doing so the project manager is led to make decisions on technical matters. However, whoever has conceived something has a great deal of difficulty in accepting any change. This is not so important for a normal project, but for a sensitive project the project manager must, above all else, be a master of negotiation. Whoever is responsible politically must never take part in technical decisions. He or she must at all times be able to criticise technical choices without giving the impression of self-contradiction. So it is quite dangerous for the IT department to install a new IT system or for the railway company to install a new rail line.

It is equally important to keep the two separate because an atmosphere of conflict is bad for decision-making. So it is easier to introduce a structural barrier between those who are on the ground immersed in conflict and those who take the important decisions. Facing increasing protest, a decision-maker must be able to make *ad hoc* arrangements, but it will be dangerous if he or she is in a position to sign lasting agreements that could be detrimental to the whole organisation at a later stage. Contrary to what people on the ground think, the project leader must not get his or her hands dirty.

By having a strong steering committee, *decision-makers will not be in the position of taking decisions alone*. Those in the front line will have to refer any decision of importance to a committee which is, by its very nature, far from the heat of battle. This will protect them and it will protect the project. As they say in chess, one must never expose the king. That is, never put the key decision-maker in a situation where he or she must manage the conflict directly. This principle has led to the downfall of many courageous decision-makers who believed they had a duty to get their hands dirty.

Fourth Method. Prepare for Conflict

The players that risk being hurt in a conflict often do not take the time to anticipate what they will do when conflict arises. It is almost as if by considering a possible conflict they might draw it down upon themselves. It is the avoidance syndrome discussed earlier. However, stress and fear are the first sources of difficulty in the management of sensitive projects. To prepare players for conflict diminishes their fear considerably and helps them to confront the situation more calmly, even if the conflict does not take place.

A contingency or *red plan* is a way of countering these problems which greatly strengthens the decision-making processes of a sensitive project.

Ensuring the Management Team's Solidarity

As the name implies, it is a series of actions to be implemented should a conflict arise (a production shut-down, no telephones, vandalised equipment, nasty letters to the newspapers, and so on). The plan outlines one or more solutions to each of these actions (training people, stand-by equipment, lists of out-of-hours telephone numbers, and so forth).

A red plan must be meticulously translated into concrete measures from the start of a project. For example:

- prepare a list of managers' direct lines which are independent of the main switchboard, and give this list to each team member;
- provide mobile telephones for all team members; and
- have detailed procedures in place to handle emergencies such as accidents.

Some measures might take more time:

- create a shift system for the IT networks;
- move some strategic services to another site; and
- sub-contract the maintenance service, which is full of opponents.

From amongst the zealots (those who are totally 'for' the project), one appoints someone responsible for security to ensure the implementation of this red plan. He or she will be flattered and the project management can concentrate on something else. It is better that whoever is responsible for the red plan is distinct from whoever is responsible for the project, in order not to clutter the mind of the latter with contentious actions which are far removed from the logic of the lateral project.

STRENGTHENING THE DATABASE

To ensure that the project team works in a coherent manner they must have the same level of information and this information must be correct. As already noted, words can mean many different things depending on who is at the receiving end. More generally, this fuzziness in words can also lead to a fuzziness in data. This happens in all sensitive projects. The more technical the project is, the truer this remark becomes. This is caused by the conjunction of three corrupting effects:

1. First, players find, keep and use data that are more favourable to their own position and they systematically forget other data.

2. Moreover, when there is a panic or when the situation becomes heated, everyone does things, says things or takes decisions that are usually forgotten afterwards.
3. Finally, during discussions arguments are often based on facts which have not been checked. A number or a fact is repeated by everyone, without caution.

These are some examples of the most important mistakes the authors have encountered:
- a so-called government decision which the Secretary of State's office had not been able to locate;
- an agreement between management and unions which, on careful reading, said the exact opposite to what the chairman had just presented to his board of management;
- an estimate of travelling time which was used in the costings of a multi-million-pound infrastructure project, which changed after being checked from three hours to six hours;
- a study which showed a major increase in the incidence of deformed foetuses following the Chernobyl nuclear accident, which has never been found; and
- the number of items a company thought it had sold which was 40% below the actual number.

From the start of a project considerable effort must be made to create and maintain a viable database, otherwise one can easily lose track of what is happening. In order to do this, let's start with two principles:

1. *Our statistics are no better than those of others.* Whilst it is important to know the numbers used by the company for its data, it is also useful to have the values which are circulating among the players. So, one does not just record the increased levels of sales calculated by the company, but also the numbers that are quoted by staff, even if they seem to be founded on nothing. Quite often both numbers are 'right', but they reflect different points of view. It is this gap in points of view which allows one to find lateralities to the project.
2. *Just because everyone seems to agree does not make the data reliable.* This is because the source of the data may not have been checked. Even among the greatest of scientists, one finds traces of selective memory which makes a helpful number 'right' and an unhelpful one 'wrong'.

Four reference works need to be constantly updated:

1. *The database of events and decisions.* From the start, a day-by-day list of events that mark the path of the project allows one to find quickly connections between facts, to put every event and every decision into context, and to know immediately, for each deadline, when it has been attained and when it is overdue. In particular, one must keep track of the decisions made and who made them as well as the deadlines agreed to and by whom.

    This database of events originates, of course, from the management of events and micro-events described in the previous chapter. It must have a direct link with the text database (see below). So, for example, if an event from the list appears as 'the signing of the salary agreement', there must also be in the text database the agreement itself. Experience shows that players have a vision of a project usually limited to the present moment. One must, quite often, put into perspective what has happened and what is going to happen.

2. *The database of documents and numbers.* It seems like common sense to suggest that one must always have assembled in one place all documents, plans and images which have been produced by the players. In particular one should have the documents which underpin the company's position. In practice, this is rarely found. Hearsay and day-to-day practice replace references.

    In order to create a database, one must automatically ask each player for their sources. For example, one would always make a point of asking lawyers for copies of the legal texts referred to in their advice. It may be discovered (as the authors have on occasion) that they have looked up the wrong reference.

    The same applies to the numbers that players use. Nothing seems more serious than numbers. In fact there is nothing more misleading. The same data might vary considerably according to how up-to-date it is. For example, the amount a company pays in salaries might – against all the odds and, in particular, against all the principles of theoretical mathematics – not add up to the sum actually paid. This type of 'real mathematics' has a natural tendency to crop up at the worst possible moment during a difficult meeting, and usually casts doubt on half of one's arguments.

    Finally, there is nothing worse than experts quarrelling, in particular when they are allies and are tearing each other to shreds on petty details. Such quarrels are all too frequent.

3. *The players database.* The list of the players in a project is indispensable as a support to segmenting the field of play. Too often a key player is discovered too late, all of which could have been avoided by a better segmentation of the field of play. There are three important aspects in creating and updating this database.

The first effort to make is to move from a nominal person to a physical person. It would be too simple and self-deluding if one contented oneself with lists of organisations with head office addresses. Nominal people have no meaning. One needs not only first names and initials, as well as the address of the person who acts for or against the project, but also some key attributes such as title, function, department, length of time with the company, and so on.

Every name will be systematically accompanied by the name of the ally in charge of each entry (this ally is defined when segmenting the field of play). *No player is left without a designated representative.* One must, as far as possible, keep track of what this person has done with regard to the project. For example, one will note letters sent or received, participation in meetings, comments to the press, and so on. The database will, for example, make it clear that a so-called new player in the debate has, in fact, been a notorious opponent from the beginning.

4. *The questions and answers database.* It has been stressed that one should not communicate widely – through media channels, for example – on a project. Yet it is important to be able to answer questions that are asked. In order to do this one needs a questions and answers database, containing the answers to the questions that the players are asking in a simple and concrete manner, and which looks at the project from the company's point of view.

One must be able to present data and answers which reflect the project's reasoning. So if a new motorway is planned, the project leader will make a map of the route. Everyone uses the same map – even the opponents who criticise it – for the simple reason that it is the only one available. If, however, this initiative had not been taken, it would have been the map of another player – possibly even an opponent – that would have been used. The principle is not only true for all visual materials (maps, plans, photos, graphics and so on), but also for all reasoned arguments. This questions and answers database must be maintained and updated regularly, with every effort made to take into account the positions of allies. The points outlined below help in the development of documents which can be accepted by everyone.

The management of databases has an important impact on the success of the project:

- It improves the *quality of perception of the project management team* and, therefore, of decision-making.
- It is a real *service to allies* who often do not have the capacity or the resolve to produce quality data. However, imposing one's own information on players runs contrary to the strategy of the lateral project, but allies will consider this as a service rendered. They have information that is qualitatively fair and correct from a political point of view, which they can use when they need it.
- Finally, these data become a source or point of reference for all the players and thus give weight to any expression.

Within the lateral project, the management of data is one of the main levers to win the support of players. Experience shows that whoever holds the information also holds considerable power of influence. For a troop of boy scouts on an expedition, it cannot be argued that whoever brought the map should lead the expedition, but if no one brings a map, then the troop is certainly going nowhere.

ISSUING REFERENCE DOCUMENTS THAT ARE CONSENSUAL

Writing, it is said, demonstrates a superior form of intelligence. However, it could be argued that it is an orchestrated intelligence which can be improved and criticised. One says of writing: 'It is written in black and white', or 'it is a thought which can be seen', or 'it can be checked'. All this is without doubt true when the following three important nuances are added.

First, *few people read documents*. Second, documents that are supposed to clarify a situation generally only present *the position of one player*. So these documents are contentious and do not clarify anything. Finally, documents are often *full of mistakes or omissions*.

However, documents should be the pillars of the project: but on the contrary they are often used as pretexts. Protest marchers take to the streets when they have never read the documents or Acts of Parliament they are protesting against. It is the same with the Maastricht Treaty which almost no one has read, and those who have are even more confused. Yet it is essential to be able to rely on consensual documents with a significant content that is understood by a majority of players.

There is no point in issuing documents that either create tensions or that are not read.

To solve this dilemma, there are simple principles:

1. Never issue a document that will anger an ally.
2. Destroy or disavow immediately any documents which anger an ally.
3. Do not defend a document criticised by an ally. Destroy it first, discuss it afterwards.
4. A document must be the result of a process, not the start of a process. For example, one will take care not to print a document as a base for negotiation, in order to get a reaction. One may not be disappointed by the result!
5. The best method to get people to read a document is to write it with them.

As it is difficult for two people to hold the same pen and even more difficult with 25, there is a process which achieves the same result relatively quickly: *the writing committee*. This system is organised in seven steps.

- *Step 1* The editor gathers a group of allies and convinces them to participate in a writing committee for a reference document. In order to do this it is necessary to outline the rules of the game and the method of work. For example, by specifying that the document need only be signed by those who wish to do so. Participation does not equate to backing the document.
- *Step 2* The editor meets everyone *individually* to prepare for the first meeting of the writing committee. This meeting allows a list of questions which the document should address to be drawn up. The first question will almost certainly be: who is this document aimed at? At this stage one would try not to answer any questions.
- *Step 3* The editor conducts the first meeting of the writing committee with two objectives: to define collectively a *list of the questions to answer*, and to agree on the *potential sources of answers*: What already exists? Where can it be found? What needs to be produced? How? As far as possible the editor should not be seen to hold the pen. If need be one will accept the text proposed by the members of the writing committee.
- *Step 4* The editor collects the necessary data and makes a first draft of a document which is issued to no one.
- *Step 5* The editor presents this draft to the writing committee at the next meeting. The document should be short so that it can be

presented and discussed in less than two hours. The text is heavily stamped in red: DRAFT, WORKING DOCUMENT or NOT AUTHORISED. Line by line the editor adds marks on the text, the comments and points of disagreement. Every effort is made to encourage the group to undertake the lion's share of the writing.
- *Step 6* The editor produces the next draft incorporating the remarks of the group. This is sent to each member individually but is still heavily marked DRAFT or whatever. Comments are taken up on an individual basis and a final document is synthesised from this. Only those concepts which do not pose a problem to anyone are kept in the final document.
- *Step 7* The document is presented to the steering committee whose agreement is sought on the final version.

POINTS TO REMEMBER

- There are several reasons why decision-making is dangerous in a sensitive project: the diversity of the positions of the coalition of allies; the fuzziness of data; bad faith and the stress levels of the players.
- To maintain allies for the project, there must be an efficient decision-making process.
- The project should be organised so that the project leader is not in the front line by:
  - creating a steering committee that is very 'political';
  - managing this steering committee by focusing it on event management;
  - keeping the project leader separate from the operator;
  - managing conflicts with several levels of players;
  - drawing up a contingency plan to prepare allies for conflicts, to simplify decision-making during moments of tension, and to lower stress by preparing players for conflicts.
- Ensure the quality of the data by managing four databases: events and decisions, texts and numbers, players, and questions and answers.
- Finally, draft consensus documents by using a writing committee.

Part V
Managing Those Who Oppose a Lateral Project

Without opponents there are no sensitive projects. The most common behavioural effect seen in a sensitive project is the magpie syndrome: focusing on opponents to the extent of forgetting one's allies and their interests. Throughout this book there has been an emphasis on a basic rule: 'To combat opponents, first take care of the allies'.

However, it is clear that this rule, however great its wisdom, is not sufficient. Everyone has an extreme environmentalist, an old retired colonel, a know-it-all, a bearded teacher, a stubborn union representative, or an obsessed scientist who systematically oppose anything that is proposed to them. If they are not taken care of, they will take care of the project.

For these opponents there are six principles of action developed by the authors which are summarised here and further developed in this part of the book:

- *Principle 1* check that the person is really an opponent, because prejudices can quickly overtake reality;
- *Principle 2* when tension is rising, master the 'daggers drawn' phase because one could quickly find oneself in an onerous conflict instead of finding a permanent solution as originally planned.
- *Principle 3* use the 'price of fish' attitude that allows a response to the attack without entering into the agenda of the opponent.
- *Principle 4* never respond collectively, individualise the answers according to the 'Horace and Curiace' strategy.
- *Principle 5* do not be deluded that an adversarial debate will lead to the uncovering of the truth. The adversarial debate is not a debate, it is a side-show.
- *Principle 6* be the white knight and attack through allies. The project's challenge is to convince passives and passives do not like aggressive people.

17 Check Whether a Player is Truly an Opponent

Our perception of players is affected by our feelings and those of people close to us. Take care not to confuse true opponents with people we don't like because of where they were born, their lifestyle, their ways of speaking or their political or other labels. This is where the sociodynamic grid is very useful: it gets away from the initial perceptions of the players and their agendas and helps to objectivise relationships.

Opponents are players who display the following permanent characteristics:

- they take practically no initiatives for the project;
- they do not look for agreements and only surrender to force; and
- their only objective is to make their own project win over the proposed project.

Our perceptions give too much importance to the antagonism of a player. But what is important for the project is not antagonism as such, but the level of initiative. For example, is this player demanding conditions with regard to the implementation of the project? To have conditions which are realistic – that is, acceptable without a total rethink of the project – is the equivalent to taking a positive initiative for the project. So this player is not an opponent. One must endure the antagonism to take advantage of the synergy.

Of course a true opponent can also make conditions for the implementation of the project: but in most cases this is 'to stop the project progressing in order to find time to reach an agreement'. Naturally nothing is offered in exchange for this concession.

It is quite common to mistake a potential ally for an opponent. In 1941, after Pearl Harbour, the authorities rounded up people of Japanese origin and sent them to camps. The United States lost determined allies and created a lasting divide with a portion of its population. On the other hand, there can be great difficulty in admitting that a player traditionally considered as an ally is, in fact, an opponent. A managing director might be loath to admit that one of the brilliant young managers – who graduated from the same university and whose career he has nurtured – is unmasked as a total opponent.

Personal feelings are misleading, not only because they give too much weight to antagonism, but also because they give too much importance to friendship. Friendship is not synergy. A friend is somebody with whom one is attuned culturally, emotionally and in leisure whereas an ally might be difficult to entertain to a dinner party. So, let's not be too demanding of our allies! In most of the projects in which the authors have been involved, their main contribution was demonstrating to the client that one of the people who was branded an implacable opponent was in reality a potential ally.

18 When Tension is Rising, Master the 'Daggers-Drawn' Phase

A sensitive project goes through a certain number of sociological phases:

1. *The 'Nirvana' phase*: the project is launched, the technical experts are in the front line, the project is on the road, everything is going well. In 1914 the soldiers went to the front with flowers in the muzzles of their guns.
2. *The 'disillusion' phase*: the first snags appear. An attack is launched on the project and it is successful, partly because not every contingency was foreseen. Mistakes are made on certain points, even if they are not yet accepted as such. Staunch allies begin to criticise the project. For example, the union asserts that the IT project is going to pose a threat to manpower levels in sales administration, when this has never been on the agenda before. One of the project engineers has mentioned this fact 'within these four walls'.
3. *The 'daggers-drawn' phase*: the conflict is inflamed and tension is rising. The knives are out and the conflict breaks into the open. Words are exchanged, fighting starts, physically or verbally. This is a key phase:

    - *Before*, one cannot estimate the true sociodynamic positions of the players. How can each player's true position be gauged when there is no tension?
    - *After*, it is too late, one is in the conflict. The critical point has been passed. Now it is not management of the project that is required, it is management of the conflict.

    At this precise moment, the tension must be lowered, even if one's allies are pressing to move forward with force. This 'daggers drawn' phase is characterised by the temptation to use power to impose the project. Among these powers, everything is possible, everything is considered.

This is a critical phase. People who are normally law-abiding citizens – including the directors of the company, but more often employees – might suggest that tyres should be slashed, phones bugged, malicious rumours should be spread or someone should be sacked. This is the level of exasperation that this type of situation generates. This tendency to enter into hostilities poses several problems.

First, he who lives by the sword will perish by the sword. It is an escalation into a high-risk strategy. The project leaders have more to lose than the opposition, or they are more conscious of what they could lose. When one chooses war, one must be able to bear the consequences of war.

The escalation of hostilities has a second fault. It favours, in the opposition camp, those for direct action, and proves wrong those (if they exist) who are ready to negotiate. Often this creates an opposition *group*, when before the conflict there were only a few scattered individuals.

Finally, the outbreak of hostilities upsets the passives. They abhor violence. Yet the objective is to have the passives in favour of the project. Passives will submit to violence and respect it for what it is, but they will never be convinced by those who use it.

In the 'daggers-drawn' phase, one must reassure the project's managers by mobilising the allies and segmenting the field of play. It is a difficult moment in which one must be able to resist the magpie syndrome and the exhortations of the hawks who disapprove of the 'hippie peace-loving' attitude taken by the project leader. In sensitive projects, true courage consists in resisting the magpie syndrome, in avoiding street-fighting or wild outbursts at management meetings. The difficulty is to hear the synergy emitted by the player, even when this synergy is hidden by a very visible hostility.

19 Fight Opponents without being Obsessed by Them: The 'Price of Fish' Response

Even with the best efforts there will always be opponents who will never be allies of the project. They will do anything to fight it. Here are some clues to identify them. *They interpret every action as a threat.* They have a natural tendency to see evil everywhere, including places where it does not exist. For example, they are invited to a public meeting to debate the issues, but they say it is an attempt to manipulate them. *They ask questions but do not listen to the answers.* Their questions are designed to destabilise, not to progress the debate. For example, they will say: 'Who will guarantee people's freedom of choice?' If a guarantee is given, their response will be: 'Ah, of course, this is proof that there will not be freedom of choice, but how are you going to compensate those people who will be wronged by you?' (implying that people will be wronged), and so on. *They do not seek to find truth, but to impose their truth.* They invite the project team to adversarial debates. The room will be full of their allies. A referee is proposed who will be biased. They offer to negotiate? They just want the project to lose time. With regard to opponents, there are two rules which apply:

1. Never let an attack from opponents pass, because the attack is heard by the passives and considered by them as valid unless it is rebutted. To ignore an attack runs the risk of leading the passives to believe that the attack was justified. As we will see later (p. 209), the best way to attack oponenents is through one's allies.
2. Never respond to an attack by justifying oneself, that is by explaining why the opponent is wrong.

How can one respond if one cannot answer? Let's take a concrete case. The head of a company presents a project to the staff representative committee. Suddenly an opponent stands up and launches into a vicious diatribe on the shortcomings of the management and their dishonesty. What can one do?

The most frequent attitudes are of three types:

- stay paralysed in the chair without saying anything (the paralytic syndrome);
- stand up and answer the accusations, one point at a time (the magpie syndrome); or
- stand up, insult the opponent and then leave the room (the magpie syndrome made doubly worse with the addition of the avoidance syndrome).

These three attitudes are obviously very inappropriate. Staying paralysed in the chair at least concurs with the principle of not taking care of opponents. However, if there is no response it leaves an appalling impression with the passives who may believe that if one has nothing to say then the opponent must be right. The same diagnosis can be made about insults and empty chair politics.

To respond to an opponent on a point-by-point basis gives weight to the questions. Whoever asks the questions leads the discussion and sets the agenda. The questions asked by opponents are not chosen at random and they are not meant to show the project in a good light. These questions are aimed at points where there are difficulties, whether the project leader is aware of them or not. To answer these questions is to give credibility to the opponent.

The correct strategy is called the 'price of fish'. The origins of this phrase are lost in the mists of time, but it is based on the phrase: 'what's that got to do with price of fish?' The phrase is closely linked to the French insult 'and your sister . . .?' which is based on a schoolyard story:

Robert, 10, has passed his school examination with flying colours. He is walking with a group of friends past Arthur, who has barely scraped a pass in the exam. Both are fond of sweet Emily who arrives on the scene. This is the dialogue:

Robert (very loudly so that Emily can hear): 'Arthur, the exam, you just made it!'
Arthur (not upset): 'And your sister . . .?'
Robert (surprised): 'What about my sister?'
Arthur (attacking): 'Your sister, she is an ugly hag . . .'

And then the fight starts, but Robert may be very good at mathematics but not so good at fighting. In this scene, Emily, playing the role of the passives in sociodynamics, would be favourably impressed by Arthur's repartee, even if Robert's attack was well orchestrated. It would be hard to say whether one or the other has won in the matter (unless there is a black eye or a cut lip), but each has preserved his interests. The 'and your sister . . .?' or 'price of fish' response does not win battles, but it allows us to safeguard our own interests.

If Arthur had responded to Robert's question, he would have entered into a dangerous self-justification. In the same way, Robert had no interest in talking about his sister whether Arthur's accusations were justified or not.

The 'price of fish' response meets an attack with an attack. It is the basic tool to use when facing an opponent. It allows one to continue without having to respond. It should be done skilfully in order to avoid appearing too aggressive: what seems fitting for young people might be out of place for older people. There are a number of ways of saying 'price of fish' which are more appropriate to the professional manager, banker or civil servant. In summary, there are three types.

The Eraser

The eraser means acting as if the question had not been heard and continuing to speak unperturbed. A company calls a meeting of staff representatives to announce a new management plan for restructuring. The union representative, a wily old fox who strikes the fear of God into the management, stands up at the start of the meeting and delivers a long speech against all new technology. He demands the setting up of a union commission charged with evaluating the changes and their effects on jobs. He rants and raves and threatens menaces and ends his diatribe with: 'What are your answers to this, Mr Director?'

The director, addressing the assembly, says: 'Well now, let's move to the next item on the agenda. . .'. He is interrupted by the union representative: 'But I asked you a question!' 'Oh, I heard, Mr Jones, and we will answer it at the appropriate time', and the director returns to the agenda. The effect is guaranteed.

The Let's Speak about It

'Let's speak about it' is a polite way of not speaking about the topic in question. There is a famous politician (and probably more than one) who is renowned for not answering the question put to him:

Interviewer: 'Mr Politician, what did you have for breakfast this morning?'
Politician: 'I had no time for breakfast, because of the appalling traffic I have to fight every morning. When is this government going to do something about the roads, what we need is investment and investment now, not only in motorways – which need repair – but also local roads. This will help the environment, bring jobs and help transport companies.'
Interviewer: 'So you had a difficult journey this morning?'
Politician: 'Yes, I had no time for my breakfast and I would like to say that the way this government treats farmers I will be lucky to have any bacon soon', and so on. . .

This technique uses one subject to lead to another subject, without any break in the logic. Ideally one would try to move to a subject which looks at the project in a positive way.

The Mirror Question

It is easy to believe that whoever speaks most says the most. This is a mistake. The person asking the questions is leading the debate. In effect, he or she sets the agenda. So, one of the most effective versions of 'price of fish' is to respond to a question with a question.

Here are some typical responses. One could start with some questions of the type:

'give me an example', or
'what about it?'

or a very impolite but very efficient

'I beg your pardon?'

This leads the questioner to repeat what has just been said. But the true objective is to lead the questioner to position him or herself on the project: by finishing on a question, one can oblige the other party to continue on a new theme.

'Mr Smith, I see that you seem to be very interested in the problem of waste, but tell me, if this waste does not go in a waste disposal site, what do you believe can be done with it?'

'Very well then, Mr Smith, if there needs to be a waste disposal site, then why not here?'

'Well Mr Smith, if it is just a safety problem, let's talk about safety. Mr Smith, what can be done to make a waste disposal site here acceptable to local people?'

In general, one should never finish a statement without following it with a question. The examples given on the 'price of fish?' techniques are taken from actual meetings or debates. But this technique is equally applicable to posters, leaflets and mailings, and to any events where the opponents have taken the initiative. One will not try to respond to an opponent's leaflet with a rebutting leaflet from the project, rather other events will be chosen as the area of communication for attack.

20 Individualise Responses: The 'Horace and Curiace' Strategy

In approaching opponents, the most classical syndrome, after that of the magpie, is the stereotype syndrome. It is best summed up by the old American saying: 'The only good Commie is a dead Commie'.

There is a national tendency to speak of people globally. Germans have no sense of humour, the French are obsessed by their livers, Americans have no culture and the British are cold. This prejudice is considerably intensified in tense situations, because conflicts caricature personalities.

One should always refer to people never to groups. *A person thinks and doubts, a group does not think and it does not doubt.* The relationships of people to people are simpler than the relationships of a group to a group. It is easier to overcome an individual than a strongly organised group. To divide and conquer is generally a bad strategy, but it is a good tactic when facing opponents.

History provides a good example of this from the war between Rome and Albe. The leaders of the cities decided to end the war, and each elected three champions who would fight to the death. The Horace brothers represented Rome while the Curiace brothers fought for Albe. Almost immediately, two of the Horace brothers were slain and the third brother ran away to hoots of derision from the crowd with the Curiace brothers in hot pursuit. Suddenly, the young Horace turned and facing the quickest of his pursuers – who had outpaced the others – killed him. Then he attacked the next fleetest and killed him too. The last Curiace, now out of breath, was dispatched even more quickly than his two brothers. This is how Rome won the war against Albe.

In the same way, when a group of opponents brings forward a petition one can turn to the third person of the second row and ask: 'And, Mr Smith, what do you think?' This will have several simultaneous and excellent effects:

- it will annoy the leader of the group and a person who is irritated often makes mistakes;
- it will trouble the person who is questioned and if forewarned is forearmed, then a surprised person is at a severe disadvantage; and
- it will show – particularly to the passives – that one is preoccupied with individuals, who paradoxically represent the common interest. The group who is organising the protest are seen as only representing particular sectional interests.

21 Do not be Lured into the Trap of an Adversarial Debate

The natural tendency when facing the opposition is to clarify misunderstandings. One says: 'we should organise a debate to throw light on the subject, by putting the opposing views in front of everyone'. This is an illusion. Putting two opponents face to face has never clarified anything. In reality, it allows everyone to dig in to their respective positions.

The adversarial debate is a debate with three parties: two parties confronting each other and one party looking on. It is not a debate, but a show, a bit like bullfighting. So one must not follow the rules of a debate, but the rules of show business. In a show the objective is not to kill off the opponent, but to win over the public. This principle has two consequences:

- The game is rigged from the start, so whoever plays fair by the traditional rules of debate loses; one must expect very little that is constructive to come from an adversarial debate.
- One must not fear adversarial debates, but must be prepared to go to some lengths to win them.

These two principles might seem self-evident, but there are numerous instances where managers have fallen into the trap of the rigged adversarial debate, where they were roundly defeated. This leads them to refuse all further debates on the ground that they are all rigged.

One should not automatically refuse all debates, but they should be avoided where possible as they take up time and time is the rarest of commodities. If one cannot avoid them, one must participate in order to win. To do this, the principle of the 'price of fish' should be used (see Chapter 19). It is important to try to ensure that allies are more numerous than opponents and, more importantly, better organised. In an adversarial debate it is the room that is the barometer of success; if the room is orderly, the passives, generally few in number, will be under the impression that the project won the debate.

It is important not to confuse an adversarial debate – which is designed to confront opponents – with a constructive debate organised by those seeking agreement, in other words allies.

22 Remain the White Knight: Get Allies to Attack

In a sensitive project the objective, as has been stressed before, is not to kill off opponents, it is to convince waverers and passives. These groups like people who succeed by being honest, nice, polite, skilful, peaceful and hard working – what are called white knights, in contrast to black knights who are evil. The best way to counter opponents without appearing aggressive or nasty is to call on one's allies.

There is a golden rule: never respond to an attack as one runs the risk of giving it too much importance or credibility. But nothing forbids one of the allies from doing so. By segmenting the roles in this way, those responsible for a project gain three benefits:

1. the allies can respond on the content and candidly attack the opponent;
2. it gives credibility to the response (since it is not the person attacked who responds, the arguments are more credible); and
3. it preserves the image of the project management, who will appear more moderate than the others since they are attacking no one. (The technique is well known to fans of romantic novels where the bad guy threatens the heroine and the good guy comes to the rescue.)

It is in everyone's interests to have a 'loud-mouth' to hand, someone who shouts out what others only dare whisper. The loud-mouth is used to retain the support of the zealots who take comfort from the strong attitude of resistance to the opponents.

In the same way, in order to comfort waverers it is in everyone's interests to have an ally – a 'fifth-columnist' – who is so close to the opponents that sometimes it is hard to distinguish between them. Both the loud-mouth and the fifth-columnist can be disowned if they go too far with their caricatures.

Let's conclude this chapter dedicated to opponents with the thought that they are never the cause of the failure of projects. It is the lack of allies that poses a threat. And it is this threat which must mobilise all the project's energies. In this book only Part V has been devoted to opponents – it is quite enough. However, some managers are more interested in swapping punches with opponents than in building a coherent project in the broader general interest.

If there are too many opponents, then the project has not been tackled in the right way. If opponents are in the minority one can feel pity for them in their isolation, but let's delegate that task to some junior assistants.

POINTS TO REMEMBER

- It is quite common to mistake a potential ally for an opponent. One must be sure of the sociodynamic positions of the players before embarking on antagonist actions which will themselves necessarily generate antagonism.
- One must be able to resist the hawks who are recommending force. The project generally has more to lose by force.
- One must never let an attack by an opponent pass, but avoid responding on the content of the attack. The secret is in the 'price of fish' response.
- To respond to the content of opponents' attacks, it is better to use allies.
- Adversarial debate is not a debate, it is a side-show whose rules must be respected in order to win it.
- An opponent is an individual. When one is facing the aggression of a group, one must respond to the individual.
- The opponents are never the reason for the failure of projects. It is the lack of allies which poses a threat, and this threat must mobilise all the project's energy.

Conclusion: Six Keys to Success

The objective of the strategy of the lateral project is to mobilise players to act on behalf of the project. This might seem like manipulation – an attempt to make people do something they do not want to do. This is not so. When dealing with complex and sensitive projects, among the first casualties are the facts. It is important that people have access to facts and the various interpretations – for and against. In a world where inertia tends to rule and sensitive projects are bypassed because they do not seem to be worth the effort, the Lateral Approach is simply a tool which allows the promoters of a project the best chance to make their voices heard. And rather than manipulation, it allows people a real say in how the project can be adapted to meet their needs rather than only the needs of the promoter.

Criticism of manipulation also comes from people who have never managed, because to manage is to solve two problems:

- getting one's staff – who are trapped in frantic but useless movement – to change their fixed views which will certainly lead to their downfall; and
- ensuring that once this change has been put in place that it is not turned on the initiator.

The strategy of the lateral project offers a concrete response to these two problems. But there is still the need to meet the following six criteria to implement it with success.

The First Key: Have a Project

In order to have a sensitive project, one must first have a courageous person who initiates it. The first courageous act is to have a rational argument on the way to attaining the objective. Without this one cannot succeed in forming a synthesis of the project. To put a lateral project in place, one must have an initial project. Too many sensitive projects are not projects, but merely representations of problems. It is easy to agree on problems, what is difficult is to resolve them.

The Second Key: Accept the Need to Rethink One's Personal Project

The second courageous act is to accept that it is necessary to rethink the original project in line with the energy the allies are ready to put into it. The art of managing sensitive projects does not boil down to the art of consensus. It is finding allies where others would only see passives and opponents and to organise them so that they act together. Consensus equals immobilisation.

To defend a point of view is already quite rare: nowadays one is highly respected for listening to the solutions of others. But if everyone is listening, silence will ensue, but progress will not. What is even rarer is that someone accepts the need to rethink a point of view. Everyone feels the owner of their own ideas: to rethink one's ideas is to rethink oneself. To succeed in the strategy of a lateral project, one must not be proud of one's ownership of ideas but be interested in the outcome.

Third Key: Favour the Individual rather than the Group

The globalisation of behaviours misleads one on reality and consequently provokes true conflicts. There has been conflict between the protestants and catholics of Northern Ireland for almost 400 years. But there are no protestants, there are no catholics. There are only individuals. To solve conflicts, one must not seek to negotiate with groups, one must seek a lateral project which will allow the mobilisation of allies from both camps. Placing the individual to the forefront in this way is neither a moral choice nor a philosophical principle. It is right because it works in practice.

Fourth Key: Favour Actions

Speech is overvalued, while the true energy dedicated to action is undervalued. Let's imagine, for example, that one is being insulted. It is not pleasant. However, what matters is what the person who is delivering the insults will do in the future. Will he or she participate in the project or not? It is better to let oneself be insulted by someone who might eventually help than to receive praise by a passive who will never lift a finger. This is easy to write, but not easy to do.

Fifth Key: Take into Account the Fears of Others

Life is change. Often people are fearful simply because they have not been reassured on their vision of the world and their anxieties have not been taken into account. One must get people to look at change without fearing it. The positive energy that some people put into projects, which they opposed just a few years ago, is a sure indicator that virtually everything is always possible everywhere, and with anyone. To help someone overcome fear is, in some ways, to share it.

Sixth Key: Bet on Goodwill

In sensitive projects (and possibly elsewhere) there are two absolutes which must be respected if one wants to succeed:

- Systematically favour people of goodwill as opposed to those who are defending their positions. A person of goodwill is not a spectator, but a player who seeks a common good above individual gain, and who is ready to rethink a position in order to make things progress.
- Have no pity for the trouble-makers. These are a small minority of people who will not change, who despise, debase and systematically attack those who do not think like them. One must, equally systematically, chase them away without pity. Not to do so would be to render a disservice to society and to the project.

There is always a majority of people of goodwill hidden behind a handful of weasels and trouble makers.

There is No Excuse for Giving Up

'Time waits for no man' according to the Bible. The times we live in must not be an excuse for doing nothing. Morally, it is not acceptable to leave future generations or one's successor with problems which could have been solved. All the more so because, technically, the time needed for change only depends on the capacity to convince.

There are efficient means to get away from situations that are felt as desperate. Whatever happens, it is better to be in a difficult situation than to give up and do nothing. It is too easy to rant and rage against the way things are if one has not taken one's courage in both hands and tried to shape them.

Some say that introducing change today is more difficult than it was yesterday: why expose oneself when people only aspire to a quiet retirement, when the baby boom has given way to the daddy boom, and when the power of the media has given the power of the censor against those who make decisions?

Yet, history has taught two lessons:

- change has always been difficult (look at Christopher Columbus);
- change is inexorable (look at Christopher Columbus).

History is eventually on the side of those who support change against those who resist it.

The authors hope they have contributed to the efforts of those who have the will to make possible and acceptable that which today seems impossible and unacceptable.

Bibliography

Berne, Eric, *What do you say after you say hello?*, Corgi, 1975.
Blanchard, K. and Johnson, S. *The One Minute Manager*, Berkeley, 1993.
Bono, Edward De, *Conflicts: A Better Way to Resolve Them*, Harrap, 1985.
Cialdini, Robert, *Influence*, William Morrow, 1984.
Crozier, Michel and Friedberg, Erhard, *Actors and Systems: The Politics of Collective Action*, University of Chicago Press, 1980.
Dru, Jean-Marie, *Le Saut créatif*, Editions J.-C. Lattès, 1984.
Fauvet, Jean-Christian, Bülher, Nicholas and Xavier, Stéphani, *La socio-dynamique: un art de gouverner*, Editions d'Organisation, 1983.
Girard, René, *Things Hidden since the Foundation of the World*, Stanford University Press, 1994.
Hammer, Michael and Champy, James, *Re-engineering the Corporation: A Manifesto for Business Revolution*, Collins, 1993.
Robbins, Anthony, *Unlimited Power*, Fawcett Books, 1991.
Rogers, Carl, *On Becoming a Person*, Houghton Mifflin, 1961.
Watzlawick, Paul, *Pragmatics of Human Communication*, Norton, 1967.

Glossary

Ally/allies. For a project at a given time, an ally is someone with at least as much synergy as antagonism, not necessarily a friend.

Animation systems. A system which organises relationships with a player or a group of players in order to increase their levels of activity.

Antagonism. This is the energy that a player develops against a project.

Avoidance syndrome. The most unconscious behaviour of a player which consists in systematically avoiding contacts with supposed opponents or with sensitive themes.

Built-in justification. This is the way individuals explain to themselves who they are and what they do and how they feel content with it.

Chrono-budget. The chrono-budget is the way a person's time is allocated in a year, a month or a week. The analysis of a chrono-budget makes it possible to identify clearly a person's attitude towards a project. Subsequently, any true change should be reflected in the way a person's time is spent.

Chrono-planning. Chrono-planning is the implementation of a chrono-budget on a day-by-day basis.

Chrono-structure. For a person or a group of persons, the chrono-structure is the sum of the chrono-budget and the chrono-planning. It is a significant representation of behaviour.

Clearing the minefield. A process of recognition by a group of the sources of tension, including personal criticisms of the project management. Once this has been achieved, it is possible to start afresh and truly communicate. This can only be successful with the help of a third party.

Communication channels. These are the ways one transmits a message and makes contact with a player.

- **Media channels.** These are direct, mass-media channels such as brochures, newspapers, advertising, television or radio, press releases, direct mail, brochure distribution, posters and company notice boards.

- **Group channels.** These are channels which involve groups such as a management meeting, a Tupperware party, an exhibition or a training session.
- **Interpersonal channels.** These are one-to-one, face-to-face relationships.
- **Factual channels.** These channels lead to formation of a direct opinion of an event, for example, a visit to a factory, training at a test site or the borrowing of equipment.

Daggers drawn. This is a stage in a project where conflict breaks out and the 'knives' are out. Social norms are forgotten and replaced by unpleasant words, verbal or even physical violence.

Desires. The energy generated by the desire for an object. It is the driving and hidden force behind our actions.

Direct (strategy). This Clausewitzian concept consists of gathering the maximum force in the minimum time to launch an attack on the enemy's stronghold and win from sheer strength and psychological superiority. Direct strategy gives all the power to planners and logistics experts. A direct strategy can work with Type 1 projects which are dominated by tasks and for which the human element only concerns resources. However, they require a clearly identified project leader who tells people what to do and who co-ordinates them.

Doing the rounds. One-to-one meetings with players where their reactions and suggestions to an initial project are uncovered. This allows one to measure tensions and to identify possible lateral projects.

Event management. Knowing of events and micro-events which might be of concern to players before they happen. This prior knowledge enables allies to be prepared and co-ordinated.

Fall guy syndrome. A behaviour which consists of blaming others instead of searching for solutions.

Field of play. This is the 'area' covered by the players involved in a project. Usually one believes that the field of play is fixed and unchangeable. If players cannot be removed, new ones can possibly be added. When defining a field of play, one should be careful not to be too restrictive. Although some players naturally impose themselves, opening up the field of play extends the likelihood of finding allies.

First circle of allies. The initial players who produce the first momentum to get a lateral project under way. The energy of the first circle of allies should pass on to new circles thereby creating other lateral projects and increasing support for the sensitive project.

Glossary

Frenetic syndrome. A behaviour whereby a player reacts to external aggressions in an excessive way. Panic rules and the player works without method, reacts rather than acts: it is a defensive position.

Golden triangles. According to socio-dynamics, the golden triangle is a group of players who have a strong and domineering synergy and a certain level of antagonism $(+3, -2)$, $(+4, -3)$, $(+4, -2)$. Concrete and technical responsibilities should be given to them. They have a fundamental role to play in the architecture of a sensitive project; they are regarded by waverers as credible in a way that no other player is.

Horace and Curiace (strategy). The principle of 'divide and conquer' based on an old Roman fable.

Human difficulty. The difficulty of a project in terms of its human or relationship content. It is the lack of allies, the abundance of passives, the presence of strong opponents and many other human factors which make a project sensitive.

Indirect strategy. This strategy makes a victory over a stronger opponent possible by attacking the enemies' weakest points. The strategy of the lateral project is an indirect strategy. It is the concerted actions of many allies which brings success. A full frontal attack could increase tensions and opposition and would probably kill the project. The indirect strategy allows allies to modify the original project, improve it and make it acceptable.

Initiative. The capacity to act in favour of a project without being asked.

Key players. See 'Players'.

Lateral project. The evolution of an initial project, based on information collected from the players, which maximises the synergy of the allies.

Machiavelli's (strategy). A style of management based on a secret society where one identifies allies, weaves a network around them like a spider's web. From the centre, one can manipulate people while remaining unseen. This strategy brings with it major faults: it creates warring clans, thrives on obscurity, shuns openness and collapses under scrutiny.

Magpie syndrome. A very common syndrome which consists of an obsessional focus on opponents. This invariably leads to forgetting allies and sometimes the project itself. The name of the syndrome originates from the behaviour of the magpie, who steals shiny objects rather than feed its chicks. Opera lovers will undoubtedly be familiar with the thieving magpie.

Glossary

Mediation. The use of a third party in order to resolve misunderstandings and conflicts.

Mediation-revelation. A five-step process which aims at creating a dynamic with a first circle of allies by opening up the possibilities for lateral projects to enhance the initial project. The basis scheme is:

- Identifying in the field of play the golden triangles and the waverers.
- Doing the rounds to collect personal feelings towards the project.
- Defining a lateral project through the information collected during the rounds.
- Organising a conference where the mediator presents to the players a synthesis of the information collected.
- Following up the first circle of allies to help them develop their lateral projects.

Micro-events. These are events which are meaningful to the players and generally overlooked by the managers. The arrival of a new photocopy machine might well be a significant event for the staff of a company and yet seem very negligible to the managers.

Moaners. According to sociodynamics, moaners have no synergy and moderate antagonism ($+1$, -2). They are passives who constantly whine. They speak rather than act. They are not allies.

Motivation/skills diagram. This is an application of the socio-dynamics grid to a particular situation. The motivation/skills diagram defines players in terms of their abilities and of their willingness to act. A manager can use such a diagram to plan training for those who have the will but not the knowledge and also to take actions for those whose skills endow them with considerable influence and whose weak motivations could make them dangerous.

Mutineers. According to socio-dynamics, mutineers have a strong level of antagonism (-4) and little synergy ($+1$ or $+2$). The high level of antagonism makes them willing to lose everything rather than let the project succeed. They will not refrain from using violence and hold extremist views.

Noah's Ark (strategy). This strategy focuses on allies (which is a good thing) and leaves others behind. Its weakness is that it evades the prime objective: to change the passives and the waverers. This is what allies can do. However, there is little point in having allies changing themselves.

Opponents. According to socio-dynamics, opponents are much more antagonistic (-3) than synergistic ($+1$ or $+2$). Unlike mutineers, opponents are sensitive to

Glossary

the balance of power and are not willing to lose everything. The rule is to ignore them. However, should one have to deal with them, one should remember that they respect certain values.

Paralytic syndrome. Abnormal behaviour by which a player, usually after setbacks, is unable to do anything. Shock sets in and even the capacity to think disappears. The benefits of a decision give way to the disadvantages only. This paralysis can easily spread to other parts of a player's work. Often this syndrome follows the frenetic syndrome.

Participative strategy. This is a classic strategy which associates people with the project to minimise the risks of opposition. Working groups meet to find a consensus. Yet, like the Samurai strategy, consensus is usually not found and if it is, it is meaningless. Indeed, opponents will use this opportunity to impose their views and raise irrelevant issues. If this strategy works with normal projects, it is not appropriate to sensitive ones.

Passives. According to sociodynamics, passives have a low level of both synergy and antagonism. They will not take an active part for or against the project, but they must be convinced if the project is to proceed. Since they represent up to 80% of the players, they clearly are the stakes of the project.

Players. Anyone likely to spend energy on a project.

'Price of fish'. Technique of contradictory debate whose aim is to face a verbal attack without responding to it. It is similar to: 'Why don't you take a running jump?'

Project manager. The person who defines the needs of the project. He or she is separate from the operator who does the work.

Retro-planning. A method which consists of starting from an objective to obtain the list of the actions required. Retro-planning is used instead of regular planning, when the objective is clear, not the way to achieve it. By listing all the tasks to achieve an objective, it isolates those tasks to be tackled first.

Revelation. The moment at which allies band together to acknowledge - as a group - their support for a project.

Samurai (strategy). The name given in project management to the strategy of launching a project as if nothing else mattered: it either makes or breaks.

Scapegoat. In its last phase the 'fall guy' syndrome changes into a scapegoat syndrome. This is when one player is blamed by all the others for all the mistakes and the errors made. Most of the time, it is the project manager. It is not necessarily a bad thing, in so far as it protects the social body. But if it is not well-controlled, it can lead to the death of the project. Well-controlled, the sacrifice of the scapegoat gives the project a new life.

Scenario method. This helps players visualise different choices. It provides a framework to bridge the gap between ideas and actions. Giving names to scenarios and discussing them brings one closer to realising one scenario or a combination of scenarios.

Schismatics. They are both highly synergetic and antagonistic. They are, at the same time, totally in favour of the project, but they also believe it is not being progressed in the correct manner.

Segmenting the field of play. Dividing players into groups so that the field of play is easier to understand and manage. The division is generally geographical, sociological or professional.

Sensitive project. One where there is complex human and technical difficulty. Also known as a Type 2 or a Type 3 project.

Sociodynamics. An analysis of individual and group behaviour, and of the laws which govern the interaction between people based on their energy levels.

Source effect. Effect on the understanding of a message depending on the person conveying it.

Stereotype syndrome. A person who fails to see people as individuals but regards them as representatives of a category with identical intentions. In sensible projects, rather than explore the complex reality of varied players, the stereotype syndrome leads one to assume that the people neatly fit into boxes and that a situation boils down to a few generalities.

Synchronisation. A phase in the discussion with a person or a group during which players attune themselves. Only then can a meaningful communication be envisaged.

Technical difficulty. The complexity of the project in terms of technology, time scales, numbers of people, financial investment, risks, etc.

Third party. An 'independent' person, who is not involved in the field of play, whose role is to change a two-dimensional discussion into a three-dimensional discussion. Third parties can mediate because they can do and say things that those involved simply can't.

Types (of project). This typology is based on the nature and the degree of the difficulties encountered in a project. Generally, **Type 0** projects reflect normal change within a company. **Type 1** projects are complex technically but not in human terms. **Type 2** projects are relatively simple technically but have a strong human complexity. **Type 3** projects are complex both technically and in human terms. Sensitive projects are of Type 2 and 3.

Usefulness. According to the VUD grid, usefulness is the conscious opinions of individuals. These opinions are rational and thus negotiable.

Values. According to the VUD grid, values are all the unconscious norms and rules individuals obey.

VUD grid. This grid attempts to represent the opinions of each player about a project according to three different and complementary levels of perception: Values, Usefulness and Desires.

Waverers. According to socio-dynamics, waverers have as much synergy (+2 or +3) as antagonism (-3 or -2). This means that depending on circumstances waverers will either back or oppose the project. Their doubts about the project are important as they reflect those of the passive majority.

White Knight. People who are perceived as being honest, nice, polite, skilful, peaceful and hard working in contrast to black knights, who are evil. The project manager has to be a white knight to get the support of the waverers and the passives. The need to respond to opponents' attacks conflicts with the necessity to remain a white knight. Hence, the importance of having allies who can fight off opponents.

Win/win diagram. A tool which helps prepare the foundation of a lateral project by identifying three types of proposals: the forbidden proposals when both parties lose something, the dilemma when one loses something whereas the other wins something, and the lateral project zone when both parties win something or at least, lose nothing.

Zealots. According to sociodynamics, zealots have a high level of synergy for the project and no antagonism. They play an important role because their enthusiasm is energy which can generate enthusiasm. However, the opponents call them 'yes men' and they have limitations: passives and waverers don't understand them, and worse, they don't believe them.

Index

1. Unless otherwise indicated, all references to a subject are in the context of 'lateral projects' as defined under that entry.
2. **Bold** type indicates an illustration.

actions, planning of   154–6, **155**
adaptation   110–11
adversarial debate, trap of   207–8
allies
  changing   39
  collective energy of   74
  consensus among   80
  in 'daggers drawn' phase   198
  definition of   216
  in example   7, 177
  favouring   66–7
  first concern for   192
  and friends   196
  helping relationship with   145–8
  identifying   68, 72, 73
  lack of, danger   210
  methodological support for   149
  mobilising   x, 73, 210
  and opponents, distinguishing   23
  perceptions of, in help relationship   148
  placing in a sector   166
  search for   17
  self-organisation, encouraging   76–7
  social dynamism of   74–5
  writing lateral projects   135–7
  see also synergy, lateral project   mediation-revelation
'animation systems' in communication channels   177–8
  definition of   217

antagonism   24, **24**, 26–7, **27**, 65
  definitions of   24, 26, 217
  in lateral project   139–40
  scale for   26–7, **27**, 86
arbitration (resynchronisation technique)   127
Arcole Bridge (Bonaparte 1796)   58
attitude of players   *see* sociodynamic position
avoidance (behavioural) syndrome   45, 50–2, 217

bank computerisation (in example)   129–30, 164–5
bank working conditions (in example)   65
behavioural change (six types)   45–6
behaviours of substitution   103
benefits
  in determining sociodynamic position   39
  moving from penalties to   139–41
Berne, Eric (PAC model)   102
Bonaparte, Napoleon (1769–1821)   58
Bono, Edward de   ix, 42, 78, 215
'break' (resynchronisation technique)   126
British Telecom, privatisation of   42

change, avoiding imperceptible   132–3
Chernobyl explosion   165

225

chrono-budget in lateral project 156–9
  definition of 217
chrono-planning 156, 159
  definition of 217
chrono-structure in lateral project 156–60
  in example 176
  definition of 217
Cialdini, Robert (cognitive dissonance) 135, 215
civil service evaluation interviews (in example) 86
Clausewitz, Karl Marie von 9, 10
clearing the minefield (in revelation/commitment meeting) 89
  definition of 217
Cobol programming *see* computer programming
cognitive dissonance *see* justification
collective action 74, 75
  see also allies
collective commitment (in revelation/commitment meeting) 90–1
collective process in management strategy 68
communication channels in micro-events
  definitions 171, 217
  media 171–2
  non-media 174–7
  types 171–2
complexity *see* difficulties
computerisation (in examples) *see* bank, insurance company
computer programming (in example) 122–3
conflict, preparing for, in strengthening project manager 184–5
conflictual way out (in Samurai strategy) 63
connotative meaning of words 130

constraints (in determining sociodynamic position) 39–41
'constructive' thought (de Bono) 42
contributions, call for (resynchronisation technique) 128
Crozier, Michel 39, 215
customer service (in example) 150–2, **151**

'daggers drawn' phase of sensitive project 197–8
  definition of 218
database for management team 185–9
  components in project management 187–9
  corrupting effect of data 185–6
  and success of project 189
  see also reference documents
'deconstruction' of players' positions (de Bono) 42
denotative level of words 129
dependency in help relationship 145–6
desires (in VUD grid) 102–3, **102**, 105, **106**, 111–13
  definition of 218
  see also insurance company
difficulties
  technical 3–4, **3**
  human 3–4, **3**
dinner party (in example) 25
disillusion phase of sensitive project 197
distribution company (in example) 12
divide and conquer strategy 205
dockers' status (in example) 75
documents *see* reference documents
doing the rounds (one-to-one meetings)
  definition of 218
  see also individual interviews

Index

door-to-door selling (in example) 136
dynamics, maintaining
  in lateral project 143–91
  in revelation-commitment meeting 91

empathy in help relationship 147
enemies 23
  see also opponents
energy *see* synergy, antagonism
EPA (French company) 8–9
'eraser' as example of 'price of fish' response 201
Euralille project (TGV) 88
Eurotunnel project 88
  see also shuttle
event management
  definition of 218
  see also micro-events
exit route (in revelation-commitment meeting) 90

'Factory 2000' (example) 76–7
'fall guy' (behavioural) syndrome 46, 57–8
  definition of 218
Fauvet, Jean-Christian (sociodynamics) 23, 33, 215
field of play
  definition of 218
  see also players
first circle (of allies) 83–93
  definition of 218
  see also allies, mediation-revelation
First World War 10–11
flexibility
  by allies' own project 77
frenetic (behavioural) syndrome 46, 54–6
  definition of 219
friends, x 23
  see also allies
future *see* view of future

Girard, René 58, 114, 215
globalisation of behaviours 53
  see also stereotype syndrome
golden triangles (sociodynamic position) 28, **28**, 29, 30–1, 65
  definition of 219
  identifying 83–4
group dynamic *see* lateral project
group meeting (in group dynamic) 79–80

help relationship (with allies) 145–8
  see also allies
herdsman crossing river (in example) 71–3
Horace and Curiace strategy in dealing with opponents 193, 205–6
  definition of 219
human difficulty, definition of 219
human element in Type 1 project 10

individual interviews
  in group dynamic 80
  in mediation-revelation 84
  see also doing the rounds
industrial productivity (in example) 6–7, 76–7
information
  and action, distinguishing between 21
  collection network for micro-events 166–8, **168**
initiative 26
  definition of 24, 219
insurance company computerisation (in example) 99–102, **100**, 104, 106–9 115–17, **115**, **117**, 170
interpersonal channels in micro-events 172–3
irrational in lateral project strategy 99–118

justification, in-built
   as cognitive dissonance 135–6
   definition of 217
   as limit to behaviour change 119–22
   structured by words 130

'key players' *see* 'players'
kick into touch (resynchronisation technique) 127

lateral project ix–x 42–3
   allies writing 135–7
   as common language of allies 149
   conceiving 99–141, 164
   definition of 42, 219
   group dynamic in 79–80
   implementation stages 149
   the irrational in 99–118
   keys to success of 211–14
   mediation by third party in 78–9
   in mediation-revelation 86–8
   moving from penalties to benefits in 139–41
   opposition to 192–214
   organised by allies 76–7
   relationships between people in 78–9
   requirement for several 77
   strategy for 71–82
   successive 124–6, **125**
   transforming to 110–11
   see also allies, mediation-revelation
lateral thinking 42
   see also lateral project
'let's speak about it' as 'price of fish' response 201–2
Liddell Hart, B. 10–11
Lyautey, Louis Hubert Gonzalve 11

Machiavelli's management strategy 68
   definition of 219

magpie (behavioural) syndrome 45, 46–9 143, 192
   definition of 219
management revolution, stages in 58
management strategies
   direct (Type 1 projects) 9–10
   direct, misuse of with Types 2 and 3 projects 11–12, 13, 218
   indirect (Type 2 projects) 10–13, 219
   that do not work 63–70
management team, solidarity of 181–91
managers
   dominated by struggles with opponents, x
   'indispensability' of, x
   flexibility in, need for 71
media channels *see* communication
mediation
   definition 220
   see also lateral project
mediation-revelation (in developing first circle of allies) 83–93, 125–6, 149 170
   definition of 220
   in example 176
   see also first circle
meeting rounds as interpersonal channels 174
micro-events in lateral planning
   definition of 164, 220
   direct contact with players in 171–3
   management of 163–78, **169**
   knowing in advance 166–8, **168**
   types of 165
mirror question as example of 'price of fish' response 202–3
moaners (sociodynamic position) **28**, 29, 35
   definition of 220
Montesquieu, Charles 139

motivation/skills diagram (sociodynamic) 150–2, **151**
  definition of 220
mutineers (sociodynamic position) **28**, 29, 30–1
  definition of 220

neutrality (in mediation/revelation) 84
Newbury By-Pass (in example) 16, 18, 74
Nimby ('Not in my backyard'), as sociodynamic change 39
Nimey ('Not in my election year), as sociodynamic change 39
'Nirvana' phase of sensitive project 197
Noah's Ark management strategy 66–8
  definition of 220
non-conflictual way out (in Samurai strategy) 64
norms *see* values
nuclear waste disposal (in example) 40–1

object programming *see* computer programming
one-to-one contact *see* doing the rounds individual interviews
operator, definition of 182
opponents (sociodynamic position) **28**, 29, 30–1
  characteristics of 195
  checking whether truly so 195–6
  dealing with 192–210
  definition of 220–1
  identifying 199
  see also antagonism, magpie syndrome
organisation, new architecture for, in efficient lateral project 132
'ostrich politics' 51

PAC (Parent, Adult, Child) grid (Eric Berne) 102, **102**, 114
paralytic (behavioural) syndrome 46, 56–7
  definition of 221
participative management strategy 64–6
  definition of 221
passives (sociodynamic position) **28**, 29, 33–5, 68
  definition of 221
penalties *see* benefits
pensions company (in example) 21
personal agenda (in group dynamic) 79
Pétain, Henri Philipe (1856–1951) 84
'players' (field of play)
  definition of 1, 221
  faults in behaviour of 45–59
  of first importance in sensitive project 15
  identifying 15–17, **17**
  as individuals 17–18
  mismanaged in example 16, **17**
  organised, importance of 74–5
  and project leader 73
  segmenting in project management 18–21, **19**, **20**, 83, 166, 174–6, 198
  in Type 2 and 3 projects 11
  see also sociodynamic position
pleasure *see* symbols of authorised pleasure
positive feelings in help relationship 147
post office (French) (in examples) 124 131
'price of fish' response to opponents 199–203, 207
  definition of 221
  examples of 201–3
private meetings
  in group dynamic 79–80

productivity *see* industrial productivity
project dynamic *see* dynamic
project formulation in Type 1 11–12
project, lateral *see* lateral project
project leader *see* project manager
project management
    traditional 1
    see also lateral project
project manager
    definition 182, 220
    separating from operator 183–4
    strengthening in lateral projects 182–5
    in Type 1 project 10
project presentation 40–1
project types *see* Type 1 project, Type 2 project, Type 3 project
purchasing centralisation (in example) 176–7

red plan in strengthening project manager 184–5
redundancies (in example) 50–1
reference documents
    consensual 189–91
    criteria for issue of 190
    production of 190–1
Renault, privatisation of 42
're-priming' of allies 145
resistance in lateral project (example of) 99–102
retro-planning in lateral projects 154, **155**
    definition of 221
revelation, definition of 221
revelation-commitment meeting (in mediation-revelation) 88–91
rewards in lateral projects 140–1
Robbins, Anthony 125, 215
Rogers, Carl (psychologist) 146, 147, 215

salary payment (in example) 55
Samurai management strategy 63–4, 69 172
    definition of 221
sanctions in lateral project 139–40
Saturn Project (General Motors car) (in example) 66–7
scapegoat
    definition of 221
    see also 'fall guy' syndrome
scenario method in reaching agreement 152–4, **153**, **154**
    definition of 222
schismatics (sociodynamic position) **28**, 29, 30–1
    definition of 222
segmenting the field of play
    definition of 222
    see also players
self-help in help relationship 145–6
sensitive project
    basic concepts 1–59
    characterising 3–14, **3**
    definition of 222
    difficulties of 181
Shuttle (Eurotunnel) (in example) 112–13
silent majority 49
    see also passives
skills *see* motivation-skills diagram
social scene round project (in generating desire) 111–12
social service (in example) 157–8
sociodynamic grid (position of players) 23–8, 27–38, **28**, 130, 195
    analysing, help in 149
    variable 39
sociodynamics
    definition of 222
    description of 23–8
sociological phases 197
sophrology (auto-suggestion) of organisations 160

'source effect' in statements   136–7
  definition of   222
'spectators'   1
staff representative committee (in
    example)   96–7
  see also trade unions
'stage' in classical projects   79–80
statistics   see database
status (in management culture)   107
  example of   121
steering committee in strengthening
    project manager   182–3
stereotype (behavioural)
  syndrome   45, 52–4, 205
  definition of   222
strategies   see management strategies
substitution   see behaviours of
    substitution
supermarket buying centralisation
    (in example)   77
symbols of authorised pleasure
    (in presentation of project)   111
synchronisation (neuro-
    linguistics)   125–8
  definition of   222
  empathy allowing   147
synergy   65, 66
  asking for help as   147
  definition of   24
  in mediation-revelation   86
  scale for   24–6, **25**, 86
  see also allies, lateral project:
    mediation-revelation
'synthesis' meetings in help
    relationship   148

team spirit (in generating desire for
    project)   111
technical difficulty
  definition of   222
telecommunications service (French)
    (in example)   124
terms, new   see words

test site creation (resynchronisation
    technique)   127
third party
  definition of   222
  see also lateral project
time, planning of, in lateral
    project   149
timing (in lateral project)   119–28
toxic waste disposal (in example)   53
trade unions
  in case study   6–7, 46–7, 48
  in phasing-in of projects   73
  school (in example)   159–60
  in segmenting a company   18–19,
    19, 20
  see also staff representative
    committee
transactional analysis   57
trial and error (in lateral
    projects)   110
Type 1 project, **3**, 172
  definition of   4, 223
  example of (distribution
    company)   12
  example of (pharmaceutical
    warehousing), **3**, 4–6
  management strategy for   9–10,
    11–12
Type 2 project, **3**, 45
  definition of   4, 223
  example of (industrial
    productivity)   **3**, 6–7
  management strategy for   10–13
Type 3 project, **3**, 45
  definition of   4, 223
  example of (nuclear waste), **3**, 8–9

unions   see trade unions
urban transport (in example)   174–6
usefulness (in VUD grid)   104–5, **106**,
    114
  definition of   223
  see also insurance company

values (in VUD grid) 102–4, **102**, 105, **106** 114, 119
   definition of 223
   see also insurance company, words
view of the future in lateral project 149
volunteers, call for (resynchronisation technique) 128
VUD (Value, Usefulness, Desire) grid 102–18, **106**, 115–17, **115**, **117**
   definition of 223
   diagnosis of player 105, **106**, 109–10

warehousing (in example), **3**, 4–6
waste *see* toxic waste, nuclear waste
Watzlawick, Paul (communications psychology) 45, 215
waverers (sociodynamic position) **28**, 29, 32–3
   definition of 223
   identifying 83–4
'way out' *see* justification
'white knights' in attacking opponents 209
   definition of 223
win/win diagram (in mediation/revelation) **87**
   definition of 223
words, new (in project commitment) 129–32

zealots (sociodynamic position) 28, **28**, 29, 31–2, 65, 75, 185
   definition of 223